Praise for *Noth*

'*A fascinating, funny and eye-opening memoir, offering a no-holds-barred account of the journey from baby barrister to Crown Court Judge. Weaving together anecdote and reflection, Nigel Lithman QC writes with compelling candour and wit, while never forgetting the most important quality in a judge – humanity. I simply could not put this book down*'

The Secret Barrister

'*Witty and delivered in highly readable light-touch prose,* Nothing Like the Truth *in fact delivers perhaps the most truthful account of a criminal lawyer's life I have read*'

Matthew Hall, author, screenwriter
and creator of *Keeping Faith*

'*Guilty of producing a very entertaining account of life as a criminal law barrister and judge*'

Lord Pannick QC

NOTHING

LIKE

THE

TRUTH

NOTHING

The Trials and

LIKE

Tribulations of

THE

a Criminal Judge

TRUTH

NIGEL LITHMAN QC

This book is dedicated to:

My parents, Dr Leslie Lithman and Ethel Imber Lithman, who set me on the right path.

My wife Debbie, the loveliest and smartest person I know, and William, Daniel and Edward, who are a wonderful part of my life.

Contents

Preface

The oath in Court:

'The evidence I shall give shall be the truth, the whole truth *and nothing but the truth*'

Will it? I doubt it.

INTRODUCTION

Bone idle thoughts

i. THE 'SPECIAL ONE'

The time is ten minutes to quiche and chips. I am sitting on the Bench in Luton Crown Court noting the Defendant's evidence, when two thoughts enter my head:

1. I'm hungry.
2. I don't believe a word you're saying.

The Defendant had been stopped at Luton airport, where his suitcase had been rummaged by customs. Two pairs of undies and a rather dubious beige suit attracted mere disdain.

The suitcase had a false bottom, like the one the Defendant is currently arguing. It contained a kilo of cocaine, wrapped in cling film and plastic, which was met with rather less disdain and ultimately led to this trial. No fingerprints or DNA were found on the wrapper. The Defendant had protested his ignorance to the police in interview, and is now repeating it straight-faced, on oath, to the Jury.

'I have no idea how that got there, I just know I didn't put it there.'

I look at him, thinking: 'I don't believe you and I haven't believed you since the prosecution first told the Jury about it.'

With five minutes to lunch, I ask myself different questions: 'Why not?' and 'Why do I think he is lying?'

My mind drifts back thirty-eight years, to long before I was a Judge.

As a young barrister, representing a person in identical circumstances, I took this line in my closing speech: 'Members of the Jury, of a hundred people charged with this offence, a hundred will tell you they were ignorant of the case's contents. Let us say ninety-nine are lying. After all, what else can they say? That leaves one person who is telling you the truth. Your problem is finding the one. How do you know this is not the one? If it just may be this one, you must acquit.'

More often than not they returned a verdict that effectively said: 'We agree. But it's not this one. Guilty.'

And yet here I am again, now on the Bench, saying to myself: 'It's not this one.'

Why not? After a lifetime in the criminal justice system, at the Bar and on the Bench, is this my default position? Was it always so?

After lunch with a Diet Coke (which, by the way, doesn't seem to be working), I come back into court

and let the Jury decide if this man is the 'special one'.
Apparently, he isn't.

ii. COUNTING ON ONE HAND

It was not the first time I'd concerned myself with the
same issue.

I don't know what you call a group of old barristers
– Queen's Counsel all. Some might say 'old farts', the
more erudite will say 'narcissists'. About seven years
ago, I was one of such a group entering the Old Bailey
robing room, the place where we change our robes
and put on our wigs before going into battle for our
respective teams, some prosecuting, some defending,
in what are commonly regarded as the most serious
crimes of the day, be it murder, rape or terrorism.

At the time I had been doing the job a mere forty-
one years. I had risen through the ranks, spending
twenty-one years as a junior barrister and then
twenty as Queen's Counsel (a 'Silk') before I was
to become a Judge. Four decades is not a particularly long time, it's just that we don't live very long.
It passes in what seems like the blink of an eye. In
fact, forty-one years is only regarded as a long time
because once we take off the years in which we drib-
ble, both at the beginning and the end of our lives,
forty-one makes up most of the rest.

On that day, and for no given reason, this question entered my head: of the hundreds of people I had
represented over the years, how many were truly

innocent? No, I don't mean how many people I had represented were acquitted by a Jury or discharged by the Judge for some technical reason. I mean, how many were actually innocent?

I had a good strike rate. I'd 'won' a lot of cases. Of course, I'd lost lots too and had some score draws (Jury couldn't agree).

I've always said that a good advocate wins all the winners, loses all the losers but wins those on the borderline. Some barristers think they are wonderful; what that says about them as people I'm not sure. I am embarrassed to mention that during one eighteen-month period representing a series of people charged with murder, the majority were acquitted. Does that mean they were all innocent? Only they and their maker know that. But Paddy Power would give me very short odds that that is the case.

Asked to approximate how many I thought were actually innocent, of all those I've represented throughout four decades, I seriously thought the answer might be such that I could count them on my fingers, toes, nose and any other handy appendage.

Now I must immediately concede I could be up to 100 per cent wrong, and I might need many more appendages.

iii. THE AGE OF INNOCENCE

It is a difficult question to answer for the following reasons. If this was a philosophical treatise, I would spend time considering the nature of innocence. It is not. I don't just mean partly innocent, I mean completely innocent. Some Defendants will spend their whole time persuading you that a part of the prosecution case is a lie. Their argument continues, if part is a lie, the whole might be a lie and an acquittal must follow.

Remember OJ? 'If the glove don't fit, you must acquit.' And acquit they did, but that is America, and having been a guest adjudicating Judge at the Florida Bar, I cannot say I am surprised. In England a Jury would have said, 'Guilty. Get bigger gloves.'

Charged with Class A drug conspiracy, the defence of one of my clients focused entirely on the question of whether a police photograph of him at the boot of a car was a forgery. It turned out it was, but that did not make him innocent of the offence with which he was charged. To concentrate on that one aspect of the case was a good tactic. If we could show that that piece of evidence was fabricated, the Jury might believe the rest could be as well. We did. They did. In fact, the rest was almost certainly a true bill.

As a barrister, I was paid to sow a doubt. Sometimes it worked and sometimes it didn't.

There's the well-known 'doubt' story of the barrister in a missing-body murder trial who said to the Jury: 'Members of the Jury, they say the victim is missing. I am going to amaze you by telling you that in sixty seconds he will walk through that door [pointing to one at the back of the court].' For sixty seconds the whole courtroom was transfixed toward the back of the court.

At the end of sixty seconds, what happened? Absolutely nothing.

Counsel resumed his closing speech. 'I told you the alleged deceased was going to appear in sixty seconds. You were transfixed at the possibility. If there is a doubt he is dead, then there is a doubt in this case.'

The Jury retired – for sixty seconds. They returned. 'Guilty.'

On the way out, the defence barrister stopped a juror (remember, it's a story): 'When I told you that in sixty seconds the deceased was going to reappear, you all gazed at the door. Even the Judge and ushers and public gallery all stared in that direction. So, you believed in the possibility. How could you say you didn't doubt the Defendant's guilt?'

The juror answered, 'Yes, *we* did all look in that direction, the Judge looked toward the door and the ushers looked towards the door and we looked towards the door ... but your client didn't.'

Trials do not deal in moral absolutes. They are not about getting to the truth. The verdict says it all. Those found guilty are said to be guilty, those found not guilty are said to be not guilty. The words used do not include 'innocent'. And whilst many Defendants take oaths in court invoking their deity to rubber-stamp their accounts, the Supreme Being in any of his guises tends to play very little part in the process. For that matter, truth does not play an enormous role in the trial process at all, and may remain as big a mystery at the end of a trial as it did at the beginning. It may upset you but not surprise you to learn that lying is an everyday part of the process.

But here I am as a Judge asking much the same question as I did at the Bar. One big difference. As a Judge I am paid neither to sow doubt nor to emphasise certainty. It's no longer my job.

iv. THE USUAL QUESTIONS

The best known question ever asked of a barrister is: 'How can you represent someone you know to be guilty?'

My answers varied, but always dodged the issue:

a 'I'm paid to.'
b 'Somebody has to.' – with a barrister representing the prosecution, and the Judge probably supporting the prosecution, it only seems fair that someone represents him.
c 'What do I know? Was I there?'

It's interesting that no one ever asks: 'When defending someone, how do you feel about securing the acquittal of a person who may be guilty?' Or, 'When prosecuting, how do you feel about securing the conviction of someone who may be innocent?' Or asking a Judge, 'How do you fairly try someone you believe to be guilty?'

I expect I am never asked that one because people are a bit cautious about asking Judges questions. But here I am so many years later, now a Judge, thinking how *do* I fairly try someone I believe to be guilty?

v. THE GOOD, THE NOT-SO-BAD AND THE UGLY

I don't think I ever met a criminal lawyer who didn't enter that part of the profession to do good and not just for himself.

The opportunities to do good are endless, both in court and in chambers and in the profession at large. That said, of course many people never miss an opportunity to miss an opportunity. And, as with all other walks of life, on every occasion we get the choice to do good or not.

For a member of the Bar, standing in the criminal courts, the positive qualities that may be displayed are dedication, integrity, fearlessness, independence, compassion and kindness, with a sprinkle of charm thrown in for good measure. The potential negatives are selfishness, greed, toadyism, endless ambition and professional sharp play.

The same opportunities are available to the Bench. For a Judge, the positives are independence, compassion, kindness and fair play. But on the negative side are the pitfalls of impatience, pomposity, bullying and bias.

Potentially, at every level, the most surprising pitfall to be wary of – and the one this book questions – is whether a cynical prejudice exists against the person in the dock. If Jane Austen had been a Judge, would she have said: 'It is a truth universally acknowledged that a single man in possession of a good fortune must have stolen it. Guilty?' If he'd been a Judge, would Benjamin Franklin have said: 'All men are created equal, and those charged with a crime must be guilty?' Had he been a Judge, would Oscar Wilde have referred to the view that any person charged with a crime must be guilty and this is the truth 'that dare not speak its name'?

Did you steal that Mars bar? Guilty.

Did you beat that person over the head with an iron bar? Guilty.

Did you beat them over the head with an iron bar and then steal their Mars bar? Guilty.

Do you believe the Complainant or the Defendant? The Complainant.

Do you believe the Defendant is innocent or guilty? Guess.

Back to my musings of that particular day whilst still at the Bar (you retire from the Bar when you go on the Bench), I asked my question of the other barristers in the room. How many truly innocent people did they believe they had represented throughout the years? Their views were even more stark than my own, and they were clearly endowed with fewer appendages than me. Someone said 'Three', another 'Two' and yet another 'One'.

vi. THE FOUR QUESTIONS

So if the belief (misplaced or not) of the advocate is that next to none of his or her clients is innocent, and it is my contention that many Judges share that same scepticism, a number of troubling questions arise:

    a How did we become so cynical?
    b Does that affect our ability to do a good job?
    c How do we cope with the pressures of working in such a fraught landscape?
    d Is the system unfairly weighted against defendants or does the system manage to ensure justice is done?

Perhaps every Judge's toilet in every court should have a poster that reads:
'Our aim is to keep the Criminal Justice system fair. Your aim helps.'

This book has a serious side. It poses some serious questions and provides some serious answers. But don't get carried away. Along the way I hope you at worst smile and at best laugh, just as I did all the way through my career.

That said, I believe my balance has always been right. Serious objectives complemented by laughter, rather than laughter complemented by serious objectives. And laughter is relevant to coping with the darkest sides of the job and our own wellbeing.

I hope by the end it provides some valuable insights into the workings of the profession and some answers to the troubling questions thrown up by that innocuous robing room playing of the 'how many?' game.

Note: There are of course some ground rules I should make clear. Most times when I say 'he' I am not being gender specific, and although I am Bar centric, any observation I make that can be applied to an advocate applies equally to a solicitor advocate. Where I have used G-d, I have done so in order not to take the Supreme Being's name in vain. (Not, I am sure, that He / she would wish to have their name associated with this book)

If you find any of the cases interesting and wish to know more, some Notes at the back of the book may assist.

I should also add that there is a fair amount of ripe blue language littered about the place, and when I say ripe blue, I'm talking stilton oozing off the cheese board ripe blue. But I am afraid the Bar was a raucous sort of place, and as much as I would like my mother-in-law to read this book without fainting, to omit the language would be to turn reality into a fairy tale.

PART I

In the beginning

I.

Pink candy

Looking back, I'd been exposed to differing degrees of scoundrel and delinquency from the get-go. I went to an upmarket school in Essex, if that isn't a contradiction in terms. This is where I first encountered wrong 'uns. The unruliest boys, instead of being sent to prison for their crimes and misdemeanours, were simply transferred either up or down the line to the next school of similar status. It was the private nature of the school that kept kids out of Borstal. As in football, the schools operated a transfer system. We got one of their arsonists in exchange for one of our boys who had burgled the tuck shop.

There was a boy at school who became a brilliant lawyer, appearing for or against the government in cases of constitutional importance. Guess what? It wasn't me. I did have ambition. In more grandiose moments, I thought I might want to be Napoleon; but really, I just wanted to stay at home watching telly.

Life peaked for me at the age of fourteen, sitting at the top of the playing fields, directing a first-year pupil to go to the tuck shop for me and get aniseed balls and shrimps – pink candy, four for a penny. It was a sunny day, without all the benefits of global warming, and I was happy. Getting a new boy to go to the tuck shop was called a sort of fagging. Today it might be called people trafficking.

Life didn't peak again until I was nineteen. My elder sister got engaged to someone who she discovered was a member of the Playboy club. Fearing he was addicted to gambling, she made him give up his membership card. He looked for someone to give it to. Providence pointed me in his direction. Fortunately for him, I was addicted to gambling and every other vice of a nineteen-year-old. The following weekend I was driving my mother's Triumph Herald for cut-price southern fried chicken and a blackjack evening looking at Bunny girls.

The only indication about what career lay ahead was in the school play. I was given the part of the Judge in Ben Jonson's *Volpone*. It was my duty to sentence Mosca, the anti-hero. I didn't bother to learn my lines. I ad-libbed the sentencing process, introducing sentences unknown to Ben Jonson or the law at that time. As you are at seventeen, so you are at seventy.

What to do when school finished?

Nothing appealed. I don't mean that nothing in particular caught my imagination, I mean actually doing nothing. These were the 1960s. The student world was afire. Protests at the Sorbonne, shootings at Kent State in the USA. But frankly, protest all seemed to me a bit of an effort.

My father's pocket money, plus holiday allowance to broaden my experience, was not going to last. I calculated that five shillings a week, properly invested, brought in £2.60 a year. The five shillings was for my first and one of my last proper jobs – cleaning his car.

I narrowed down my options. I got places at university to read Oriental Studies – appropriate in two ways. First, I was interested in the Middle East and, second, I've always supported Leyton Orient. I spent six great months at the Hebrew University in Jerusalem. Fascinating but perhaps not the makings of a career. Mossad didn't come knocking (apparently unlike us they don't recruit spies from universities).

It was back to square one – what to do?

The options left were the law and teaching. The law ran in my family. Those who couldn't stand the sight of blood became lawyers. At one stage, I used to boast that our family represented the whole legal spectrum. There were two barristers, a solicitor and even a stenographer (before proceedings were taped). But there was always a deficiency. You spotted it. The Lithman household was missing a Defendant. Fortunately, a distant relative came to our rescue. I shan't say how. Bingo – full house.

Teaching was the more worthy, but for breaks, coffee, smoking and generally posing, the Bar seemed unassailable. I chose the Bar. How to set about it?

First stop Chelmsford Tech. I have always been very proud of the fact that I went to a technical college, encouraging youngsters that you can go to a tech and end up a Silk and a Judge, you don't need to go to Oxbridge. Mind you, if you get the choice – go to Oxbridge.

2.

The Inn crowd

The traditions of the Bar included selecting and joining one of the Inns of Court, and as part of the qualification came the tradition of dining a number of meals per term. You dined in messes (groups) of four, and each mess had a bottle of sherry, a bottle of red plonk and a bottle of port. If you were fortunate enough to dine with one or two teetotallers, there were spoils aplenty.

This was the Inner Temple. Thanks to Stephen Solley QC it had accumulated a fine wine cellar so large it would never be exhausted and so valuable that the good stuff would not be wasted on scrotes like us.

A group of us used to meet and dine together. Again, I experienced someone with a 'bit of form'. She was an outlandish woman wearing thigh-length red boots. I asked her what had made her choose Inner Temple. I had joined as my cousin was a member and it had a nice big car park.

'I joined because of my conviction,' she said.

'What do you mean?' I asked. 'Do you think the Inner Temple has the highest moral standing of the four Inns?'

'No,' she said, 'I was done for shoplifting at Woolworths and the Inner Temple didn't seem to mind.'

Drunken driving had not been heard of then, and whilst now we say 'don't drink and drive', back then we used the old adage 'having a jar, take the car'. The students tended to be divided between those who had never started to drink and those who couldn't stop. I remember in the 1970s you could leave the Temple and turn right toward Westminster by going through the gap in the middle of the road. On one occasion I had to get out of the car and walk into the middle of the road to see if the gap was still there. Somebody appeared to have taken it away. There is drunk and blind drunk. This was ironic, considering I was later to be asked to prosecute for the campaign against drunken driving but, as between the ages of thirty and fifty I was not interested in alcohol, it was not inappropriate. Nowadays, I have returned to my roots and am rarely without a single malt by 7 p.m. or, as we call it in North London, allowing for time differences, 5 p.m.

The 4.30 train from Chelmsford Tech to Liverpool Street transported barristers from Chelmsford Crown Court back to town. There was a dining car and drinks bar. These barristers in black jackets and pin-stripe trousers carried blue bags or red bags, badges of the Bar. They contained wigs and robes and connoted seniority. Today they have been overtaken by wheelies, the sorts of trollies those intent on stealing from Asda might take.

The other badge of the Bar is found amongst QCs. In the summer months, instead of a suit to work, they would often wear a cream jacket and dark trousers. A friend of mine used to call it the 'Silk at C&A' look. But what made the barristers on the train impressive was that they were clearly able to afford gin and tonics and had lively, futile conversation.

I met my first big beast on the train. Anthony Scrivener QC. I engaged him in conversation.

'You're a barrister, aren't you?' I asked. 'Can I be one?'

'Certainly,' he replied. Recruitment was quite tough in those days.

As it happens, I didn't go and see him to get a pupillage (training place). I went instead to a country house weekend in the grounds of Windsor organised by the Bar to give you a look at what you might be signing up to. There I met a woman who suggested I come and chat to her. She gave me the choice of a pupillage with her or the son of the Head of Chambers (subject to interview). Not being entirely stupid, I plumped for the son.

I was interviewed by a man who, being unfair about it, had every appearance of a Nazi. He had a shock of blonde hair, a clipped voice and I could see my image in his shoes. I thought I recognised him from the movie *The Boys from Brazil*. I had not met a true Aryan previously and I am not sure he had met a Jew before. It was probably like that part of the Woody Allen film: I saw him as having a swastika armband and he saw me as having side curls and dressed top to toe in black. Neither of us were that far out.

3.

Playing the odds

I joined a set of seventeen barristers. They took three pupils per year to learn the trade, one to whom they offered a permanent place (tenancy). Very good odds by today's standards. My two rivals were probably better than me but had professional self-destruct buttons fit for suicide vests.

The seventeen of us would meet after court for tea at 4 p.m. Some would discuss the cases they were doing. Pupils remained silent. I did for two reasons. First, I didn't have a clue what they were talking about, and second I concentrated on the ginger nut biscuits served with tea. I have always been a martyr to my ginger nuts. When I took up my appointment as a Judge, I spread the word that all of my pals were welcome to come to my room at court provided they brought their ginger nuts with them.

On day one, as Donald Trump would have called it, the Head of Chambers, Tony Cripps QC, a really lovely man whom it fills me with warmth to remember, asked the assembled company about a particular case he was doing. The question he posed was based on title rights to property. I recognised some of the words, like 'house', but by and large the topic was one with which I had not even the most cursory under-standing. All seemed flummoxed until one of my rivals offered up his opinion. Right or wrong, pupils did not have opinions. That was him out of the running. My chances were now 2–1.

Day two. My other rival came to tea wearing no jacket and smoking. That was him done for. I was now the evens favourite to be offered a tenancy by those chambers. I knew all I had to do was turn up for six months and I would be in. Mind you, that didn't make it a certainty. I didn't cock it up.

The Chambers, 1 Harcourt Buildings, was a family business. I did pupillage with Seddon Cripps, the son of the Head of Chambers. Had I not been his pupil, Seddon was the sort of man I wouldn't have plucked up the courage to speak to. He was about 6'6" and an Old Etonian. But, I hope like all members of the Bar, the relationship between pupil and pupil master / pupil mistress (now called Pupillage Super-visor) is very special. On my first day in court with him, I plucked up the courage to suggest that after the court hearing we should spend lunchtime at the Angel riverside pub in Henley having a debrief on the events of the morning. The sun shone, the debrief was brief and the next year with Seddon began to look very rosy.

My Pupil Master was clever and confident. His work, that I had to prepare, was beyond my ken.

One set of papers I thought it best to drop behind the radiator in the room which I used with him and his next pupil Dominic Grieve. That is the Dominic better known as the MP who created much difficulty for Theresa May. Had I foreseen this, I would not have shared my ginger nuts with him and would have dropped his work behind the radiator as well.

Chambers had two QCs – Tony plus one very large and kindly person named 'Fat' Griff. He enjoyed taking young members of Chambers for an evening out. His favourite invitee, Charlie Gratwicke (later to become the head Judge at Chelmsford Crown Court), was unavailable one night and the mantle fell on me. These evenings were always the same: American Bar at the Savoy for cocktails and champagne, followed by Kettner's restaurant in Soho, where champagne continued to accompany dream dishes. Suddenly, I was reminded why I had opted for the Bar. 'Have what you like and sign for the bill,' were his last words as he made for the airplane that awaited on him to take him to Wales. I did not require a second invitation as clearly the I.O.W. in his initials stood for I Own Wales.

4.

Rising to the challenge

In the second part of pupillage, I went to court alone. Early days at the Bar involved getting up at the crack of dawn and getting to court early to meet the client and get the feel for the court. Like a team coming onto the pitch to see how it would play.

These days as a Judge I wake up at the crack of 9.15 a.m., set off for work at 9.30 and I'm in at 10.12 ready to start at 10.15. I'm considered lazy. I don't agree. I often don't leave court until 3.45 p.m., in time to get home and watch *Pointless*, a gameshow named nicely to encapsulate some of my work day.

The Resident Judge (administrative head) where I sit is the marvellous and very patient Michael Kay QC. He actually doubts I sit as a Judge at all. As I'm the last one in, he doesn't see my car arrive, and as it's the first out of the garage, he doesn't see me depart. He has no reason to see what I do in court all day, so he only sees me at lunchtime. As my conversations at lunchtime are entirely non-legal and, indeed, often illegal, he really does wonder what I bring to the party. I have suggested sandwiches. It was his job to delegate different responsibilities to us Judges. One got providing summaries of the most recent criminal cases from the Court of Appeal. One got responsibility for technology and dealing with those Defendants to be categorised as recidivists. I got catering.

But in the early days at the Bar, I was the first to arrive at court. My first chambers did a mix of what was called Common Law, that is Family Law (whingeing spouses), Civil Law (arguing the toss about property) and Criminal Law. The problem with family and civil was that the cases never seemed to conclude, whereas in crime the cases involved a stricter timetable and a clear result. After all, these were upright, no-nonsense villains.

I had gone to the Bar to do Criminal Law, to defend the inalienable rights of people to be as dishonest as they wished. There was a matter-of-fact straightforwardness about them. By the time they reached you they were blessed with a degree of desperation. My favourite county had been Essex, where I had been 'educated' and aspired to live. But Essex has some very different parts, and I started my professional life going daily to Grays Magistrates Court. Grays was a particularly poor part of the county, with a mix of pawnbrokers and pound shops (in those days 75p shops) – and attendant crime.

The police were not then constrained by the rules of the Police and Criminal Evidence Act 1984. They made their contemporary notes of arrests, independently together, back at the canteen over a Bovril or on the back of cigarette packets:

'And after I cautioned the Defendant he replied,

"Fxxk off, I ain't done nothing,'" which I took to mean fxxk off he had done nothing, "'and you can't prove a thing,'" their notes read, as the ink continued to dry. All of which the Defendant denied.

The magistrates accepted the word of the police nine times out of ten. In fact, also on the tenth time.

Trials were heard in the Magistrates Court of quite serious cases. After about four months in practice, I went to Grays for my usual scrap with the police. Invariably, the defence was that the police were lying about everything.

They said my client had bashed one of them. The reason they said that was because they knew that a policeman had actually bashed him. The police strategy was to turn defence into attack. This was one of the ten times where the magistrates preferred the account of the police. I thought the maximum penalty would be a fine. He was sentenced to six months in prison. I suddenly thought, this is really rather serious. This is not a game.

The more serious crimes went to Chelmsford Crown Court. Life was equally cavalier there. A woman charged with assaulting someone said to me: 'That policeman said if I agreed to sleep with him, he'd drop the charges.'

'What did you tell him?' I asked.

She adopted an exaggerated air of extreme hurt that I should need to ask her. 'Certainly not.'

I only asked in the forlorn hope I might get home to watch the cricket.

5.

Essex, not ethics

Essex of course is the East End made good.

It can be broadly divided into two. Beautiful rural northern Essex – including Thaxted – the village I lived in for many years, 'England's prettiest village' according to John Betjeman – and the less opulent or picturesque south. Whilst Gustav Holst had written *The Planets* in Thaxted, Ronnie and Reggie Kray, the leaders of gangland London, also hung out in the county. Essex was a haven for crime.

Whilst all of London crime went into a dozen or so crown courts, the best known of which was the Old Bailey (Central Criminal Court), effectively all of Essex crime went into only two centres, Chelmsford and Southend. So Essex was a great place to practise.

There was a part of crime folklore which involved a visit to the property of an Essex villain, a few miles from where I lived, in search of silver bullion stolen by a gang in a robbery. The gang who had committed the offence came down to retrieve their ill-gotten gains and threatened that if they weren't told where they were hidden then the lady of the property would be murdered. It appears the response from the husband was 'Well, I am sure you know best.'

By the 1970s, 'Essex man' seems to have developed from *Homo sapiens* into 'Jackus the laddus'. Jack had a particularly flexible view of the truth. A case that summed it up as well as any other I can think of was that of a forty-year-old James Hunt lookalike I represented. He was charged with manufacturing a drug that was an amphetamine lookalike. 'Jack' had been offered some to sell and was a little surprised when two tons of it turned up. He had been outing it by the shovel-load but, ultimately, despite a Christmas Sale he was left with a massive amount on his hands. He buried it at his farm in Essex.

He was charged with offences under the Misuse of Drugs Act, but the authorities had not done their homework. This was not a proscribed drug, and so they could only succeed under the Medicines Act, much to the annoyance of the Judge, who, having got hold of a pharmacology book, wished to throw it at the Defendant.

'Jack' was a pretty cool guy, but I was amused at how he brought out his old flared trousers and floral shirt for the trial. He usually wore Savile Row but thought coming down-market was a good idea. He went to prison for six months. Had it been Class A it would have been twenty years.

He was also charged with striking one of the officers who came to the farm, and kicking his car. In a moment of enlightenment, but only after the trial at which he pleaded Not Guilty, 'Jack' was overcome with an urge to tell me what really happened. 'Of course, I didn't hit him. For five hundred quid I could have had him murdered.' He paused and then added as an aside, 'but I didn't 'alf kick 'is car.'

6.

Loyalty

It could never be said that the good people of Essex aren't loyal to their own. Word had it that when jurors were called for Jury service at Snaresbrook Crown Court on the edge of Epping Forest, they would listen to the charge sheet being read out, and when it dawned on them that they were not implicated, they would breathe a sigh of relief. Now, the test for dishonesty in the rest of the country did not seem to apply to Snaresbrook. The Jury inevitably acquitted the Defendant. He then having no conviction would find himself on a Jury and the process began again.

At that court I prosecuted, unsuccessfully, a character from the soap opera *EastEnders* – known as Ricky (actor Sid Owen). The only thing Ricky/Sid was guilty of was being a celebrity in the wrong place at the wrong time. He was alleged to have struck a clubgoer at the Epping Forest Country Club. He admitted it, but said that he was responding to a man who had struck him first. He had been the one targeted due to his fame. This was self-defence.

In support of his defence, Ricky (Sid) – or was it Sid

(Ricky) – called as a witness the make-up girl from *EastEnders*, who produced video clips from before and after a particular episode. She said in the after shot you could see Ricky had a fat lip from where he'd been struck. As the prosecutor, I suggested to the Jury it could not be seen and that this was a case of the Emperor's new clothes. Being fairly literal in Essex, they could not understand why I was referring to Ricky (or Sid) as an emperor. Anyway, short story long, having called the older Mitchell brother, Grant (or was it Phil?) to attest to his good character, he was duly acquitted.

I finally despaired of this case being taken seriously when the Judge after the Jury's acquittal turned to Ricky saying: 'What happens to Phil and Sharon?'

Still, at least I got Phil's autograph – or was it Grant's?

PART 2

The inside track

7.

Blind justice

It may surprise you to learn that there is at best a flimsy relationship between justice and truth. I know they should be, but they are not bedfellows in the criminal justice system.

A client came and saw me in chambers.

'I'm looking for justice,' he proclaimed.

'In that case you'll be wanting the chambers next door. I don't deliver justice,' I helpfully replied. 'If a favourable result can be obtained, I am as likely as anyone to deliver it. But I don't deal in justice.'

It is not as glib a comment as first appears. In cases where fatalities have occurred, whether they lead to Defendants charged with murder, manslaughter or death by dangerous driving, being convicted, no penalty, however harsh, will bring a loved one back. People who have had their life savings stolen will not have them restored. Some do recognise this from the off and their definition of justice changes. It morphs into the simple desire not for revenge but for an open hearing and recognition of what has happened.

I hesitate to use the word 'unique', but such were the combination of facts in one case. On a given day, two men, both graduates one from an Australian University, appeared in different magistrates' courts in Essex. As a sort of Essex boy myself, I hope you'll forgive me for observing that it's rare enough for two graduates from anywhere to find themselves in Essex at the best of times, and this turned out not to be the best of times. They were both charged with an identical offence, indecent assault on different women in different parts of the county. They both had mental health issues. They were both remanded in custody and held in the same prison. The overlaps were spooky, as was what was to happen. Ridiculously, and one can only hope not malevolently, they were put in the same cell.

One beat the other to death.

Both sets of parents came to the county for the autopsy and the inquiry that followed. In the mayhem of the attack, one had bitten off the ear of the other. He had bitten off more than he could chew – but marks showed he'd had a go. Despite the horror, the victim's parents were sad but sanguine. 'It could just as easily be our boy who killed yours,' they said to the other parents. This was pure bad luck. And in a way it was and nothing could bring back the deceased. Neither set of parents was concerned with innocence and guilt, just what the authorities could learn from the episode.

There was an inquiry into the murder; I doubt anything emerged other than the forlorn hope that lightning rarely strikes twice.

8.

Perjury and porkies

We all know the phrase 'Lies, damned lies, and statistics.' Whether it was Mark Twain or the British prime minister Benjamin Disraeli who said it doesn't matter. The Criminal Justice system is founded on one statistic. In a hundred per cent of criminal cases someone, if not everyone, tells lies. The courts are full of lies and liars, and that's before we start counting the lawyers, or Heaven forfend the Judge.

In an early part of my career, I recall exchanging an affidavit on behalf of my client with the opposing lawyer in a family law case. He approached me with his document in his outstretched hand saying: 'Here are my lies, in exchange for your lies.'

Of course, in a Jury trial, one side always tells lies. The system depends on liars. It would fall apart without them. The consequence of lies are clear: if a Jury believe the Defendant is lying they will convict; if the Complainant is lying they will acquit. Lies are part of the process linked to the success or failure of the party charged with the crime. It does not even have to be the lies of the Defendant himself that does for him. It may be lies of people he calls to give evidence on his behalf. Why would they be lying if he is innocent?

But, I hear you say, what about perjury? When you tell lies in court doesn't that make you a perjurer? You may be right more often than you expect. The reason that not every case leads to a perjury trial is not because fundamental lies haven't been told, but because the cases coming before the courts would immediately double if each case led to another prosecution. And this is notwithstanding just how big some of the lies are that we hear. Orca big, as they say in *The Usual Suspects*. It was only right that in one case that I prosecuted I suggested that notwithstanding telling the Jury how he had had his teeth knocked out, the Defendant still seemed able to lie through them.

Because of the issue of a burgeoning number of cases, if every case were to lead to another prosecution, the country's case load would double. How is this resolved? In practice, where the lies would raise issues of public policy such as a lawyer or police officer lying on behalf of another, the Judge will refer the case to the Director of Public Prosecutions for him to consider whether prosecution for perjury is in the public interest.

Perjury is invariably linked to perverting or attempting to pervert the course of justice, and the courts take an intolerant view of it. In any case where a lie might lead to an individual suffering imprisonment or avoiding detection – e.g. a false alibi being provided, or a false allegation being made that might lead to a charge – these are likely to lead to perjury charges being brought. In other words, mere porkies are forgivable, perjury is not.

The person who fabricates a rape allegation undermines true complaints of true victims. The driver prepared to take the points of their spouse can lead to a dangerous driver remaining on the road. These are the sorts of crimes that undermine the system and that Judges come down on like a ton of bricks – with prison the usual outcome.

As with all criminal sentencing, there is guidance to try and achieve uniformity of approach when considering the gravity of the perjurer's conduct. How long the lie was persisted in will have a bearing. For example, if a false rape allegation is persisted in both before and at trial, the Defendant is likely to be remanded in custody and, if convicted, faces a lengthy stretch. The consequences of maintaining the original lie are severe.

So, once on the bench, notwithstanding her being of impeccable character, I felt compelled to send a woman in her fifties to prison having been convicted of providing a false alibi to a murder suspect. You just can't go around giving accused murderers false alibis, even if, as it turned out in this case, the alleged murderer decided to jettison the alibi and use a different defence.

Put simply: when a person embarks upon such a course, they do so at their peril.

As I have said, there is a difference between perjury and porkies. A guilty Defendant will invariably have to lie to escape justice. But even they can go further. Predicated by the sheep and lamb principle otherwise more colloquially referred to as 'shit or bust', the Defendant's behaviour can sometimes lead to a different category of serious conduct: witness intimidation and Jury nobbling.

On the intimidation front, a third party may approach a witness and offer to invest in the Defendant's acquittal. What might be bought is either a bit of amnesia or it used to be that whilst a little more pricey, of all the places a witness might go to on the day of the trial, that should not include the courthouse.

But an irony has arisen, particularly since 2003. The law permits a witness's statement to be read if it turns out he stays away through fear. As it is the statement that condemns the Defendant, it might be money better spent making him attend!

You might think that poor behaviour is to be expected from Defendants; after all, what else has brought them before the courts? In practice, criminal clients are, for the most part, easy to get on with. Likewise, it benefits the smooth running of a trial if the Judge shows the Defendant both courtesy and interest in his welfare. If a Judge treats the person in the dock well, they will rarely repay that respect with mischief. That said, it's unwise to leave any doubt as to which of you will be going to prison, if called upon to do so.

Of course, a Defendant's behaviour cannot be guaranteed. In a gang trial I oversaw as a Judge, it was brought to my attention that some of the Defendants were smuggling drugs into the custody area. This was being done via special grooves dug into their trainers. Once this was discovered, the police took over and, ultimately, the Defendants were not just sentenced by me for the gang crime but were later tried in relation to the drugs. Their trip to prison was a shoe-in.

I guess some Defendants do what some Defendants do. They are the embodiment of the fable of the scorpion who hitches a ride across the swollen river on a frog's back. Halfway across he stings the frog and as they both begin to drown, the frog asks, 'Why?' The scorpion replies, 'It's what we do.'

9.

The Rolex and the ring

Lawyers tend to steer clear of behaviour that can bring trouble down on them. They are aware of the rules. They tend not to get into bed with their clients, either literally or in terms of colluding with them to invent a story. Very few can claim to being amoral. So whether they obey the rules is a matter for them. But their instinct tells them what the rules are and makes them largely compliant. An underlying fear of being reported to their disciplinary body and being 'taken off the road' (suspended from practice) does the rest. I also rather quaintly believe that integrity is the advocates' fallback position, and few are dishonest.

I have had only two occasions to 'complain' of lawyers' behaviour: once at the Bar and once from the Bench. I know nobody likes a snitch, but where the behaviour is reprehensible, something has to be done. Removing an exhibit from the courtroom without the Judge's permission is a good example. I was the Judge.

The true reasons for lawyers' compliance can also be more pragmatic: why would anyone risk their career for someone facing criminal proceedings? And win, lose or draw, they will be paid. So, by and large, the Bar is not corrupt.

At the beginning of my career, when I was still wet behind the ears, my client sidled up to me saying, "'ere. Five 'undred quid if you can get me off.' As a young barrister I felt terrified that I could be doing something wrong, and so went and told Judge Greenwood at Chelmsford.

His reply: 'Go and tell your client you're going to try and get him off anyway and to stop being a cxxt.'

So I did. I went out and announced to the client: 'Judge Greenwood says I'm going to try and get you off anyway and to stop being a cxxt.'

Twenty years later the same sort of thing happened again. One of my pals from the profession was a big Scouser with all the cheek and charm that would see him through this life and the next. We'll call him Tom, although that is only half his name. By this time, I was a QC and was brought in to lead Tom in a case in which our client was supposedly paying for our services. That was the theory anyway. We had been promised that he was good for the fees, right up until the court hearing. But when we arrived at court the client said he was waiting for money to arrive into his bank account, but would we proceed on the trust that it would materialise?

I explained to him that whilst he might think he had us over a barrel and we would represent him even if not in funds, in fact the Bar Council Rules forbade us from going into court unless the case was either legally aided, privately funded or pro bono (being done free and gratis). Tom thought Pro Bono was an Irish band leader and did nothing that way. As funds had not arrived it was none of the above, and I said to the client we couldn't professionally represent him. He asked for the case to be delayed a day and the Judge agreed. The money was on its way from Spain.

The following morning, Tom and I met the client around the coffee machine outside court. It felt like illicit meetings with school friends behind the bicycle sheds for a fag.

'Well, what is the position?' I asked the Defendant. 'Are you able to fund the case? Otherwise, we must withdraw.'

He went into begging mode. 'Please, please, I know the money will come, just start this case. Here, I will give you this Rolex watch and signet ring for security.'

I pulled myself up to a full 5'7" and, looking at D, said: 'I'm sorry, Sir, I am one of her Majesty's Counsel, not an effing pawnbroker.'

As I was finishing the sentence, I felt a tug on my gown. 'Eh, eh,' Tom was saying, his accent being fluent Stevie Gerrard, 'that's great jewellery, that is; you take the watch, I'll take the ring.'

I resisted the very untempting suggestion. It felt like we were either in Hatton Garden or Romford Market, both places in which Tom felt at home. Just to make you realise I am not that snotty, I am more of a Brick Lane kind of guy.

Ultimately, the money arrived and into court we went. I cannot remember the result. That is not selective memory, it is just that whilst I am not blessed with instant recall, fortunately, I *am* blessed with 'instant forget'. The moment I finished a case I invariably forgot it. Instant forget allows you to clear your mind of the case you have just finished and make room for the next.

But it wasn't all so intense. The fact is that every courtroom scene could also be entertaining, and many I found funny. Tom the Lively Lad was not the only style available as a barrister. Others tried the same but without his charm or polish. This is an example.

An advocate (Barrister A) was appearing in a cut-throat murder trial. They are called 'cut-throat' as two Defendants each blame the other for the crime. (They don't actually involve any throat cutting, though of course they may.) The Jury is presented with a choice that if it was not the other man charged with murder then it must have been his client. But it is a fiction that the Jury will only choose one to convict. The reality is that more times than not they will convict both.

The two advocates representing the Defendants had big egos. I (with a slightly smaller ego) was defending a third Defendant and my hope was, that, like Harry Houdini, whilst the Jury were engaged with the other two, my client would sidle out unnoticed. Let us say the Defendant being represented by Barrister A was called Keith, because that was his name.

Barrister B repeatedly said to the Jury it was not his client, it was 'that killer', Keith. Again and again, 'not my client, but that killer, Keith'. Keith's barrister (A) naturally complained to the Judge. This was not evidence, nor was it fair. It merely tarnished the name of Keith. By constant repetition. The Judge agreed and, upon being told off, Barrister B said he would not refer to him in that way again. When the Jury returned, he said to them, 'I've been told not to refer to "that killer, Keith" as "that killer, Keith", and, having said I won't, of course, I won't. So, what I will do instead is refer to "that killer, Keith" as "TKK". Every time I say "TKK" you will know I am referring to "that killer, Keith".'

The Judge put his head in his hands.

Result?

Keith: Guilty.

Other Defendant: Guilty.

Yes. My client did sidle out between them and, no, that is not why I told the story.

10.

Making merry

As I hope is becoming clear, the Bar and legal profession is the most wonderful way to spend your day with your clothes on – if you don't play golf. On the other hand, if you do play golf, you will particularly enjoy one of the examples below.

If you have a sense of humour, it can also be the most wonderful source of fun. But that said, it is fundamentally an insecure profession. You are only as good as your last brief. You spend your life thinking you will never be instructed in another case again. It is fiercely competitive, and rather than acknowledge that there is work for everyone, it can bring out the worst in some – and I emphasise *some* – in whom the characteristic of smug self-satisfaction can pervade.

Ridiculous, really.

After all, 'What is one drowned barrister on the ocean bed?' 'A good start' – and, let's be honest, whilst a surgeon could do our job, we could not do theirs.

Having said that, this is not so serious as to preclude fun. My father was a consultant anaesthetist, and during operations would sit at the sharp end of a patient – his head – feeding breath and life with one hand whilst doing the *Daily Telegraph* crossword with the other. It is perfectly normal to take things perfectly seriously on the one hand and perfectly frivolously on the other. I would not be the only barrister to have played Brick Breaker, Snake or Candy Crush on my phone whilst listening to mountainous and monotonous schedules being trawled through.

That does not mean that both my father and I did not experience horrors. The difference is that, whilst mine existed mostly on paper, his were first hand, added to the fact that whilst he could have done my job, I could not do his.

But don't get me wrong, the Bar is a perfect place for the fertile puerile mind. It's not by chance that we resort to gallows humour, and that is not reserved to the time the condemned were waiting their turn on the gibbet. Some of the stories I heard as a young-ish man were literally gallows humour: Henry Green QC, whilst a Junior, was left by his leader to finish a murder trial in which they had been appearing for the Defence. The Defendant was convicted and the Judge had donned the black cloth atop of his wig in the tradition when passing a death sentence. As his leader had gone to appear in another trial, Henry had gone to see the client. What to say to a man just sentenced to death? Some platitudes were followed by an awkward silence. Finally, on leaving the cell, he offered this advice to the client, 'Well, just keep your chin up.'

Fortunately, not all acts of humour were at such profound moments, and many no doubt occur as part of a coping mechanism to what was going on. Mind you, some are just downright funny.

Here are some first-hand silly examples that I (no doubt wrongly) found entertaining.

The Judge always knocks twice: It is customary to stand up when the Judge enters. That is preceded as a warning by the usher knocking firmly twice on the door through which he enters. I never tired of the things I used to get up to even when others did (after all, repetition is a quintessential part of comedy). In the old courtrooms at the Old Bailey, I found that rapping knuckles twice beneath the desk produced the exact sound the usher would make. So I knocked, everyone rose and a moment later groaned.

Nativity: Christmas was drawing near and I was involved in a murder at the Old Bailey. The lawyers were seated at their benches behind upturned boxes with dividers in which to place their files. My Junior and I had no files; we were doing this case paper-light, an eye on the Amazonian rainforest. But the boxes and dividers were tempting us. We got a box with dividers from Ryman. What to put into it? In the quieter moments of the trial, we brought in bits of straw, some model animals and a figure or two and created our own nativity scene.

Join the club: Humour rarely stayed the right side of the appropriate line in what you might refer to as the case of the murder and the golf club. Not the Agatha Christie-esque *Murder in the Golf Club*, but 'Murder with *a* golf club'. My junior and I represented a man in his thirties, who had the misfortune one day of being telephoned by his sister. 'I've just got off the train,' she said, 'and there's a guy here who is looking at me really pervy and it's quite clear what he's got on his mind.'

Our man started to get into his car to show the fellow what *he* had on his mind. As he went out the door, being a keen golfer and finding it to hand, he armed himself with his putter. He alighted at the station and, sure enough, there was a man hanging around both the station and his sister. Our client would not have been selected for the diplomatic service or to negotiate at the end of World War I. No, what our client did was swing the putter in an arc, the shape of which put the club through the eye and into the brain of the man who had got off a train shortly before and shortly after became the deceased.

As far as tactics went, our submission to the Jury was to admit there had been an unlawful act (the station did not have a putting green, so it could not have been an accident), hence it was at least manslaughter. But the fact that he acted spontaneously, using an item not obviously designed to cause serious injury, meant the Jury agreed he did not have the requisite intention for murder but was guilty of manslaughter. A score draw result.

Our team went off very satisfied with the job we had done. Over lunch in the Old Bailey Mess (canteen), debate was lively about whether our client would have been better to have used a number seven iron or a three wood.

The old man and the splint: A sad, lonely man used to frequent a working men's club. He befriended a number of other men there, who generally availed themselves of his generosity. The older man had more than drinks on his mind. Being in his late seventies he had had an operation the likes of which I was unaware. He had a splint inserted into his penis that provided the appearance of being in a state of permanent arousal. Two younger men took him home and, after robbing him, murdered him. I appeared for one of them. What stays in my mind are the post-mortem photographs. The victim was laid out on a table with a sheet over him. It had the appearance of a graph. For virtually all of it, it was a straight line, but if that line represented the months of the year, there was an unexplained spike around October.

Last example (thank goodness, I hear you say; change the subject).

Nobby's Nuts: Even the most teetotal of readers is familiar with the brand of peanuts sold in many pubs. During a murder trial, a witness recounted how she had gone into a pub and there seen the killer sitting at the bar with a drink in his hand and a packet of Nobby's Nuts. In olden times, the Bar was always blessed with a solicitor's clerk, sitting behind us, taking a note of the evidence. This was usually a reliable, ready reckoner as to what precisely was being said at any given time. The clerk, sitting behind us and between us and the Defendant, could go to the dock at the back of the court and ask our client for his comments.

At about the time this witness was giving her evidence about Nobby's Nuts, I noticed the clerk's attention wandering, and decided to strike. 'Could you go and ask our client who Nobby is, please?'

She woke herself up and went towards the back of the court. Halfway there she worked out what was happening and turned back. As she arrived, she whispered through gritted teeth, 'You bastard.'

II.

Making money

I have never met a criminal lawyer or barrister who went into the job for the money. The majority of them would have gone into it with a strong social conscience to help others. People might go to prison. That's not a good thing. People get hurt in the course of crime. That's not a good thing. Can I help sort this out, please?

And that's the way things start. Money, if there was any, would be a bonus. In my first chambers (I had two), I went to work and a long time later I got a cheque. Work ... cheque, that was the system. Work, cheque, work, cheque. But the cheque was not for the work I'd just done but for work done a long time previously. The cheque would be put in a blue book with the name of the case it applied to copperplate-written by our clerk. For the 1970s, the chambers were unusual in that they employed a female clerk, Eileen, although usual then (now antiquated) in that she was paid a percentage of the barristers' earnings rather than a wage.

But, oh joy, when, at the age of twenty-four, at the end of the week the blue book had a cheque in it.

Later, I was one of a minority earning a lot of money, but in the early days that was not any part of a motive for work; I wanted to sort out people's lives. I had come to the Bar to help people. Now, suddenly I was getting paid, and the more cases I did the more I earned. Binge-earning became like binge-watching Netflix or binge-doing anything and, whilst I didn't do it for the money, being able to afford a vanilla cornet with a chocolate flake in it was better than only being able to afford one that did not have a chocolate flake in it.

That was meant to be figurative, but in Southend a '99' Rossi's ice cream with a flake in it was better than any other. They do make the best cornets in the world. 'Rossi' had also given me an eye opener. One of my holiday jobs had been as a post boy at Trower, Still and Keeling, solicitors to the posh.

'Nigel, deliver this package to Mr and Mrs Rossi,' came the order.

Great, I thought, day trip to Southend, thinking Mr and Mrs Rossi were bound to live on the Westcliff sea front. How could the Rossi family, however wealthy, live anywhere except by the ice-cream stand on the sea front? The address took me to a penthouse flat in Curzon Street, Knightsbridge. Of course, it may not have been *the* Rossi family. But, hey, this is a book – and anyway, where there's ice cream, there's brass.

I was also quite good at the job. Speaking isn't much to be proud of. After all, the first human heart transplant was performed by Dr Christiaan Barnard, not by a barrister. But I was getting cases from both sides and all sides. The police realised the way to spike my guns was to instruct me themselves, and as my coffers got fuller, the '99s' ended up with hundreds and thousands on top.

All of the work was in Essex. I lived first in a two-up-two-down cottage in a village called Ford End, and then in a lovely country cottage in Thaxted. I began to work hard and well, and learned the truth of the mathematic equation: the harder you work the luckier you get and, I guess, the more you will earn. And don't ignore luck. I would rather be represented by a lucky advocate than a good one.

That said, it's not binary.

I was building a close relationship with the police. Not only did I appear for those alleged to have gone awry before their disciplinary tribunal, but I would deliver talks and lectures to them.

At one such talk at Q & A time a policeman put up his hand and asked as follows:

'Mr Lifman [Essex police for 'Lithman'], we hear that you earn £60,000. Is that true?'

I answered, 'I have to be honest; some days I do and some days I don't.'

The paths to renumeration at the Bar are varied. Once a reputation is forged – if there is a clamour, however small – clients who can afford it will pay privately to do so, and rates can be high. And so top lawyers, be they barristers or solicitors, here or abroad, may earn top dollar.

But, be it in medicine or law, remuneration is problematic, especially in the earlyish phases, which can last for many years. And it continues to be a problem when the public purse is repeatedly cut so that only the most privileged can afford to enter the profession. I will come back to this later in a chapter entitled 'Taking on the government'.

A well-known comedian was asked, 'What's the secret of staying married for a long time?'

'Don't get divorced,' he answered.

The secret in those days to being well-remunerated at the Bar was to have more than one case on the go. It wasn't greed. Or certainly not *just* greed. For me, it was largely tied up with needing to believe I was popular, both as an advocate and a person, that made me move from one case to another. I received a lot of ribbing on the topic, some gentle, some dull. To go between cases was how Silks operated through to quite recent times. Consultant medics do the same. I suspect the criticism also crossed professions – my father would see someone before and after an operation and, of course, during it. Thereafter, he would see them twice a week, say Tuesday and Thursday. I used to ask him what happened if they died on a Wednesday? Reply came there none.

I have been reminded of many of the stories in this book by people who were there. On one occasion

I had two overlapping trials at Croydon and the Old Bailey. I had Juniors in both who enabled me to keep these plates spinning. I arrived at Croydon one afternoon to find my Junior, Kieran Galvin, speaking to our client. Slightly out of breath, having rushed from the Old Bailey, I greeted both of them and let Kieran continue.

'Don't worry, although Mr Lithman has another case running, he will afford you 110 per cent of his attention.'

That next moment the client looks around and there are just two of them.

'So ... where's Mr Lithman now?' asked the client.

'Gone back to the Bailey,' said Kieran.

PART 3

Cops and robbers

12.

The bad old days

The historic relationship between the police and villains laid the foundation for the cynical view of a Defendant's guilt.

In 'the old days', whenever they were, a Judge's sympathy for a Defendant was as rare as ... well, you just choose your favourite simile. Before 1898, a Defendant was not allowed to speak in his own defence. Oh, heady days. How many professions include the thought, if only we didn't have clients?

The only real question then was, 'Has the prosecution made you sure of his guilt?' If so, you the Jury must say guilty, and me the Judge must sentence, whether it be a fine, prison or death, and of course try not to get them muddled. Judges learned that the only side of the case was the prosecution's and, hence, every murder trial was a short step from the gallows or deportation. With only one team allowed to play, the game was over much quicker.

Murder trials now take anything from, on average, a week or two to a month or two. Back then (whenever then was), it was a day or two. I remember in the last twenty years a colleague renowned for his quick wit, Gilbert Gray QC, being reprimanded by the Judge for the time the case was taking:

'Come, come, Mr Gray, this murder trial so far has taken six weeks; in the old days it would have taken two weeks.'

Back came Gillie, 'In Iran it would take two hours. Doesn't make it justice though, does it?'

During the 1960s and 1970s, policing standards dropped. If you wanted to know the time you used to be able to ask a policeman. Now you were on your guard. In Paris they said that in the 1960s, if you wanted to know the time and you asked a policeman, he was just as likely to rape you.

The reason for the poor reputation in England, as well as abroad, was the police view that they were fighting crime with one arm tied behind their backs. The 1980s Battle of Orgreave between the miners and the police created images on TV that shocked the nation about police behaviour, and views became polarised. Different police units likewise contributed to divergent views of the police.

'Sweeney Todd', the Flying Squad, initially comprised two horse-drawn wagons patrolling the streets with officers hiding inside, ready to pounce. It became known for action-packed takedowns of armed robbers known as a 'pavement ambush', and got the name Flying Squad because it operated across London without adhering to borough policing boundaries. Interesting that a hundred years later we are still talking about 'county lines'.

When I began to work in serious crime, organised police were on one side and organised armed robbers – 'blaggers' – on the other. Like duellists, each side would draw weapons for the day. Both teams were relentless and unyielding. The police were effective but cut every corner possible. They produced notes of observations – 'obs' – as to what the 'baddies' did whilst 'on the plot'. Their notes might be correct or just as easily invented over a cup of tea in the canteen. The defence counsel (often with reputations as 'blaggers' briefs' that dogged their careers) made swingeing allegations of corruption against the police, some well-founded, some not. The courtroom was the battleground.

And then came the concept that there could be real miscarriages of justice and people could be 'fitted up'. Police records made up, false confessions, as crime got more serious so did the ruthless steps taken to combat it.

And that is the genus of the notion that, in a court of law, you were really on one side or the other. There grew a close alliance, albeit not a corrupt one, between the Judges and the police on the one hand and the villains on the other. As a lawyer, you either advocated the truth of the police or sought to expose their lies. Long ago as an advocate it was very rare for a prosecutor to defend, and vice versa. As a Judge, it was second nature to support the police.

A Judge would hear a mini-trial in which he would be asked to rule upon evidence said to be inadmissible. It was a complete waste of time. The officer would swear by his account and the Judge upheld its truth. How could he do otherwise?

Once learned, could such lessons be unlearned?

13.

The pace quickens

The year 1984 brought a change: the Police and Criminal Evidence Act (one giant PACE for mankind) introduced codes of practice to regulate arrest and interviewing. It was the Custody Sergeant now who had charge of the prisoner, not his arresting officer. The arresting officer was no longer free to go to the cells and see the suspect for a cosy little chat.

Things did change, but it was taping and then videoing of interviews that really began to ensure fair play. Now the battleground between cops and robbers had shifted. A policeman could not fabricate evidence of what the Defendant said in what was called 'the verbals'. It was recorded. Telephone evidence, cell site analysis, DNA, this was how crime was being detected.

But more importantly, the nature of crime changed. Why risk your neck trying to rob safety deposit boxes of thousands of pounds of valuables when you could commit the crime on paper and steal millions? No guns.

The fact that goods could be imported VAT free and then sold on in the UK with VAT, which was never repaid – i.e. 'knocking the VAT man' – gave a whole new meaning to crime. 'Missing trader fraud' led to vast reclaims of VAT, and millions were paid out by HMRC to smart villains. The same goods went round in a circle between companies that 'traded' for a little while then ceased. The same money moved likewise. The only thing that moved in reality were forged invoices. Nobody got shot.

As the years have passed, the police have been perceived differently. I suspect that, if you asked the public what they believe is the answer to our wicked society, they would conjure up a scene reminiscent of the 1880s. 'More police on the street,' they would cry. The Victorian peelers is the era we long for. Steel caps on cobbled stones. Whistles. Pounding the beat. Chasing after Jack the Ripper.

The utopian view of policing is now largely irrelevant. Police on the beat is not an answer to terrorism. It may be an answer, but intelligence and cyber-policing is probably more relevant.

14.

Heroes and villains

I have dealt with all ranks of officers in all sorts of courts and all sorts of disciplinary hearings. 'They' speak of poachers and gamekeepers; I'm never sure which is which but, having built a reputation for successfully defending criminals in Essex, I was recruited by the police to represent them.

I started at the top, with the Deputy Chief Constable of Essex, the second most senior police officer in the county. An animal rights protest group were blocking the small Essex town of Brightlingsea to prevent cattle being loaded onto a boat and exported. The DCC gave the go-ahead for the laden lorries to go through a no-entry road. The protesters brought a private prosecution against the DCC. It was symbolic, in the sense that it would be a feather in the caps of the protesters if the DCC could be shown to have acted unlawfully.

It was an interesting experience to watch three local magistrates hearing the case. Would they find against the second most senior policeman of the county? Of course not. Did they? No.

The defence was the dubious one of necessity. Necessity had been held not to apply to murder by dint of cannibalism where the occupants of a marooned lifeboat had decided to kill and eat the galley boy. But driving down a one-way street was *probably* different.

Whilst I had my doubts as to whether this was a defence that could be generally applied, I need not have worried. The sight of the officer in his uniform, 'scrambled egg' on his arm connoting rank (as opposed to me, who had scrambled egg on my waistcoat connoting breakfast), medals, wearing gloves and carrying his baton, meant the result was never in doubt. The Magistrates decided that even if cannibalism was broadly frowned upon, you should be able to drive your vehicle the wrong way down a one-way street if it was necessary.

And so, in the good county of Essex, my prosecution practice expanded until it was maybe 50/50 prosecution to defence. A chatty, easy relationship with my clients was divided equally between cops and robbers. I suppose I was a bit of a tart.

The role of the police meant they fell into one of two categories. The heroes were those who put their lives on the line to protect our society. The villains were either the criminals they brought down or the rotten apples in the police barrel.

The enmity between the police and their suspects could be unforgiving. I represented a man for firebombing a policeman's house whilst his wife and kids slept upstairs. Make no mistake, this was war.

I also never understood who is supposed to be who, but as often as not I was on the side either of the angels

or the villains; in other words, I would sometimes prosecute and sometimes defend, although you'll be relieved
to learn never in the same case, and in Essex there was
a time when I was instructed on one side or other in
the majority of serious crimes being tried there.

Police and thieves played cat and mouse. The
'intel' in such cases is enormous, and they resemble
icebergs. Part of the information is there to be seen;
the remains languish under the waters.

In fact, there were not just two teams hanging
around but four. There were the police who behave
like police, and criminals who behave like criminals.
Next were police dubbed 'rotten apples', who behaved
like criminals, and finally there were criminals
who behaved like police (for instance, using anti-
surveillance techniques and equipment employed by
the police to see if they were being watched).

Whilst some barrels of officer apples had a worm
or two in them and some were beginning to turn, few
were actually mouldy. But it was quite difficult to tell
if the apple you were dealing with had a brown spot
on the outside or a maggot on the inside.

The problem for them arose when they had to use
force to quell a turbulent suspect. They could use
reasonable force in the execution of their duty to arrest
those where there was a reasonable belief that they'd
committed arrestable offences – but whether these
suspicions were well-founded was a moveable feast.
Contrary to popular belief, the police had enormously
high standards in relation to disciplining themselves.

15.

Reg 7

Unlike their shoes, the one-size regulation seven fitted all police officers.

It was a widely drafted regulation designed to meet almost everything a policeman could do wrong. No one ever knew what rules 'Regulation Seven' referred to, it was just 'Reg 7'. The protocol was, if a policeman was thought to have taken a step out of line, get a senior officer to serve a Reg 7 disciplinary notice on him. Then, if the server of the notice seemed to have stepped out of line as to how appropriate it was to serve the Reg 7 notice, they would get an officer senior to him to serve a Reg 7 on the server. And so on and so forth. Reg 7s were the confetti of the police service, and it was hard to find a policeman who hadn't had a Reg 7 served on him.

But all of those served were entitled to a hearing, and all were represented by a lawyer, so this became a not infrequent and not uninteresting part of my practice, as the following tales illustrate.

MINDING YOUR PS AND QS

P and Q were two Essex officers who ended up in a pickle barrel. Two more different individuals could not have been found. I represented P. There were, of course, many more letters to his name. The officers had been charged with dishonesty and improper behaviour in the house they had been searching (the 'drum' they had been 'rolling').

The police officers, somewhat eccentrically, decided that a small amount of cannabis in the house probably belonged to themselves, and at the same time, if the person whose house you are searching happens to be selling knock-down shirts, it might be appropriate to buy one. They were hauled up before the Chief Constable. Somehow, they both managed to achieve results that enabled them to go back into the force. P chose to do so. Q's work ethic was so strong he had spent his time whilst awaiting the hearing selling second-hand cars, and was far better at that than police business.

Essex police were like everything else in Essex, larger than life.

Sergeant L also got himself into trouble for entering a suspect's cell to subdue him. He was the highest-ranking officer of those who did so. The force that can be used and the blows struck are set out quite specifically in the regulations. Knee strikes and the like have diagrams saying, 'Don't try this at home.' He ended up being tried for assault in the Crown Court before a Jury and then tried for a disciplinary offence in front of his chief constable, and to the best of my recollection he was acquitted of both. There was a very senior and totally blameless officer involved in his prosecution. Needless to say, he had a Reg 7 served on him.

In the barrel were plenty of other apples. One Granny Smith we had better refer to by the initials G.S. He had been a senior police officer in the north of England, a part of the country at the time policed in accordance with what was referred to as 'zero tolerance'. G.S. probably should have guessed that zero tolerance extended to a court exhibit – allegedly stolen from the police property cupboard, having been recovered from a burglary. Call me an old romantic, but when the officer gave it to his wife as a birthday present he might have cleaned off the fingerprint dust. Nevertheless, the Jury could not make up their mind as to his guilt. Nor could the next Jury. As it used to invariably be the custom that one retrial was the maximum a Defendant would face, he left court without a stain on his character, even if the dust had left a stain on his wife's dress.

So there were rotten apples, but by and large police were fighting crime.

Unless of course they were committing it.

THE COMEBACK KID

Whatever else you could say about the police, they are never short of a quick reply. When it comes to an exchange between two masters of the dark art of banter, they are as two jousters at the pass. This exchange was at Southend Crown Court:

Barrister: I was just suggesting to you that your notes are fabricated and your evidence a lie.

Policeman: I understand that, sir.

Barrister: I suggested the same thing with a policewoman witness at the Old Bailey last week.

Policeman: Oh, yes, sir?

Barrister: I don't suppose you even know where the Old Bailey is, sir.

Policeman: I believe it is in the City of London.

Barrister: I made that police witness cry.

Policeman: Oh, yes, sir?

Barrister: Yes. I frightened her.

Policeman: Oh, yes, sir?

Barrister: Do I frighten you, officer?

Policeman: No, sir. But you would if you were representing me!

16.

Bobby the bobby

Bobby featured in my first murder trial. I was nervous as we entered Chelmsford Crown Court about an hour before the trial, to be greeted by the officer in charge of administering the case – Bob. But what followed was a little unconventional.

We expected our team (as was customary) to be served with last-minute documentation. In fact, we were served with eggs. Bob, who did a great impersonation of Basil in *Fawlty Towers* and had John Cleese's bobbing from side to side down to a tee, had brought some eggs in from the hens in his garden and was trying to sell them.

'Eggs? Wan' any eggs, Mr Lithman? 'Alf a dozen – free range? Eggs?'

'Er, not really, Bob, thanks.'

I'll never know whether this was a genuine performance by a genuine eccentric or just a way to disarm the defence.

This was one of those cases that will always stick in my mind. Memory is such a strange thing. Some cases I could relive minute by minute and some are gone for ever. It isn't surprising that my first murder trial still looms large, particularly as it took place at Easter time. There are three reasons for this.

a. I really enjoy every aspect of horse-racing. When it comes to betting, I often say that 'I follow the horses'. Then I add, 'Mind you, so do the horses I follow.'

The trial centred on a killing that occurred on Grand National day. An older man lived with and was looked after by a younger man. The younger one had selected a bet on 'Grittar', who ultimately won the race. He asked the older man to put his money on down at the bookies. The younger man should have made a killing. Unfortunately, he did.

They settled down to watch the race and saw 'Grittar' win. Only after did the old man confess he had forgotten to put the bet on. If this book teaches you nothing else, sometimes honesty is not the best policy. He was beaten to death by the younger man.

b. The younger man's defence, flimsy as it was, was that although he had delivered a couple of blows, the Defendant had then left the house. A stranger must have entered in his absence and finished the old man off.

I was a very young barrister and, sadly, I was led by a dithery Silk. He failed to take the one point we had. There was a trace of blood on the victim's sock. This must have meant that he was still alive after the first beating and trodden in blood. It would have made no difference, but the point was not forcefully taken – in fact, I cannot recall if it was taken at all.

c. As a racing fan I also backed the horse. I got 7–1 for Grittar. The Defendant got 20–1. Twenty years for one murder.

17.

Top of the cops

Dick was an Inspector at the sharp end of crime. He was truly involved in a war. He wasn't exactly Dirty Harry, but he knew that to take on the enemy required a reasonably elastic view of fair play. He had seen too many people escaping justice for no good reason. But this is my surmise. My actual relationship with Dick was based on mutual respect.

I first met him in a conference with my Junior and solicitor. He did not deal with bullshit well. Unfortunately, this was the *spécialité* of my particular *maison*. The times I had gone into conference having read somewhere between some papers and no papers were too many to recall. It has been called 'winging it'. I had a PhD in winging it. It was not that I was lazy, I was just sometimes too busy with too many briefs on the go at the same time. Somebody once drew a caricature of me in court. He had me holding a brief with the name of the current case on it on my desk and in my hand another case which was awaiting my attention.

Usually after the conference starts you can ask a question like, 'Well, how do *you* see the issues of the case?' The person in the conference will then enlighten you as to what the case is about.

Unfortunately, 'bullshit' and 'winging it' were not part of Dick's vocabulary.

'What do you think the main issues of the case are?' I probed.

He looked at me long, hard and cold. 'I'm not here to find out what *I* think they are,' he replied. 'I know what they are. I'm here to find out what *you* think they are.'

He was a heavy-set man of about 6'4" and, like a police dog, was trained to sniff out 'bullshit'. My Junior was terrified of him, and I was not much more comfortable. He fixed me with a stare that did not break. I wish I had been to the same school of statecraft that he had. He had learned never to speak unless and until you have something worth saying, and preferably not even then. What he managed to convey was just how serious this business was. If he wanted to speak to a chatty clown, he would go to the circus.

His Sergeant Graham was the iron glove on Dick's iron fist. They worked as a team and brought to the case everything that helped Essex citizens sleep at night, and Essex citizens like me to sleep during the day. They also taught me how loyalty was a two-way street. Whenever they had a serious case where they needed a QC, although they could shop around, they would use me. I was loyal, and trustworthy, and believe I always have been.

Tragically, but as is so often the case, Dick's fall from grace was as spectacular as his career. Having been in the frontline for so long, he himself ended up, after a stress session with the bottle, before the Magistrates. I was only too happy to both represent him and provide him a reference. It could not professionally save him.

The last of the triumvirate was WPC Pauline Foreman, what we used to call a policewoman, but is now called a policeman. It is now PC to refer to a woman PC as a PC. Like the others, when appropriate, she maintained a sense of humour.

This story may cause consternation, but when she learned that one of her 'repeat customers' of the criminal fraternity had collapsed and had a heart attack, she sent a card to the hospital, saying, 'I was sad to learn that your last arrest was cardiac.'

These were frontline, serious, crime-busting policemen. Who would not but side with them in their fight against crime?

By way of a postscript, following his leaving the police force, Dick decided to qualify as a criminal solicitor and set up shop in Essex. He was pretty much as successful a solicitor as he had been a copper. Landing on my desk, shortly after it landed on his desk, came his most important case, of a woman charged with poisoning one of her children. It became probably the most interesting case I have done, and I have set it out a little later.

PART 4

The middle ages

18.

LOMF

It began to dawn on me that the people amongst whom I moved professionally – namely, Defendants – seemed to display a certain Lack of Moral Fibre (LOMF).

The higher I climbed the less there was.

As I became more senior in chambers, I did more work in the Crown Court. The brushes with morality became clearer and the question more earnest.

For example, I represented two crew members from an ambulance. They had ignored a radio call to attend a road traffic accident and, to disguise their laziness, had driven the ambulance to a side road, parked and cut its fan belt so they could not attend the emergency.

How could people be so immoral? How could I represent people I knew to be guilty?

I was busy. That's why. One brief ended as the next began. I was on the work treadmill.

The elements to a criminal trial are that the Prosecution opens the case to the Jury (tells them about it), calls each witness, whom the Defence cross-examines, the Defendant usually gives evidence and both sides make a closing speech, then the Judge sums it all up and the Jury decide.

Whilst the Jury are deciding, the next case begins. If you defend in case 1 and prosecute in case 2, they can follow one after another, endlessly. And so the treadmill begins. Get on it at your peril.

Like Hotel California, 'You can check out any time you like, but you can never leave.'

19.

Something in the air

Having demonstrated an association with delinquency from the earliest days, I pose these generalisations as questions: are people intrinsically evil? Are places?

Within northern Essex, chocolate-box village scenes would belie a slightly weird underbelly. One of the villages was known as the 'Village of Death' – Coggeshall. At the time, I was living in Thaxted, itself a fairly peaceable place. As the world centre for Morris dancing, it seemed likely that the worst thing that might happen was to be hit by a tambourine. But Coggeshall and other towns came with different labels.

Within a very short space of time Coggeshall had attracted its nickname due to three murders that had taken place in or near it.

Jeremy Bamber lived in Mersea and was convicted of murdering his family at White House Farm. He was tried at Chelmsford Crown Court and as the trial proceeded, we shared the same subterranean corridors often at the same time and in the same direction: he on his way to Court 1, me on my way to see other clients in the cells below. But for the last two hundred years the Bar has stalked the corridors with those who are in the public eye for reasons other than altruism.

Coggeshall's second murder was committed by the owner of an antique shop. He too duly appeared for trial at Chelmsford. My only link with him was thus. I owned a cross-bred border collie, Tinker, and one day whilst walking him, he squatted and did what dogs do at the entrance of the antique shop where the murder had taken place. This preceded the common use of little poop bags, and all I can do, thirty-five years later, is take this opportunity to apologise to the owner who, frankly, had enough problems as it was. Allowing Tinker to do this, I accept I put my foot in it. I just hope nobody else did.

The third killing was of a woman who disappeared from the Village of Death. I say killing, as this was based on nonstop gossip in the local pub. She had certainly disappeared. It occupied more time in the country village than a storyline in *The Archers*. At one stage, in seeking her murderer, the front gate where she had lived was taken 'into custody', to see if it could tell a scientific story. It didn't. No arrests followed. Does it follow that nobody was killed?

Indeed, I have appeared in cases where none of six Defendants jointly charged with murdering a woman were convicted. I used to wonder if nobody killed her, why is it that the last time she was seen, she was lying on the floor with a knife protruding out of her back?

But what about Coggeshall? Was there something in the water? Did it attract crime or the accusations of crime? It was well known that places around there were famous for witch trials, where logic and justice were turned on their head to obtain the demise of the alleged witch. If they immersed a suspected witch woman into a lake and she drowned then, as her soul had gone on its journey, she was clearly innocent. Dead but innocent. If she did not drown and hence her soul was rejected, she must be guilty and was then executed.

Just run that by me again.

20.

White van man

Not all Defendants are the personification of evil; many fall into the 'There but for the grace of G-d go we all' category.

In these cases, we transfer from the question 'How can people do such wicked things?' to the other imponderable, unanswerable question, 'Why do bad things happen to good people?' Happenstance plays its part. One sunny day in June, two German tourists were walking parallel to the Thames where the hill upon which the Monument to the Great Fire of London stands. On that hill, facing downwards, was parked a white delivery van. At the bottom of the hill were bollards making the road a no exit. The bollards kept the pedestrians safe. The white van had the usual, old-fashioned handbrake. As it was pulled up either the button, pressed down at the end, lifted it seamlessly or it was taken up, click by click, through its ratchets. As it passed click five out of eight it bit and the brake held. Unless it did not. On this occasion it was not tightly applied.

The driver had parked momentarily, to deliver a parcel to the large building sited on the road at right angles to the hill. The tourists were in a happy mood and walked in and out of the bollards at the foot of the hill. Fate had decreed another car would play a role. A Volvo came out of the road on which the building stood. It turned right, up the hill. It clipped the van. The van handbrake loosened. It hurtled down the hill and, as the tourists turned in rather than outside of the bollards, they were pinned and crushed to death. Their city break was coming to an end in any event. At home, their loved ones received their remains.

Meanwhile, white van man – who was actually not behaving anything like white van man – was both distraught at what he had done and very upset that he might be incarcerated. He escaped the verdict of manslaughter but was convicted of a lesser charge. The Judge did not send him to prison.

21.

'The horror, the horror'

Mumbling these words, Marlon Brando earned nearly a million dollars in *Apocalypse Now* for a few hours' work.

The courts too traded in horror; the only difference is that what happens in court is not just acting, it's more real than that. And it became part of the baggage that occupied and influenced me as I moved into the senior ranks of the profession and later on to the Bench.

The horror in which I traded was on paper, in photographs and, ultimately, in the form of live evidence from victims, witnesses and Defendants. Some were head-on and some more subtle. Having appeared in over 100 murder trials, they too came in every shape and size.

In the 1970s, all murder briefs were accompanied by all of the post mortem pictures showing all of our insides in glorious technicolor. I was once asked if I would like to attend an autopsy as part of the defence preparation. As the defence was 'alibi', I politely refused.

By the time I came to routinely appearing in these cases I had been appointed a QC – I hope I am not teaching my grandmother about silky knickers, but a QC is also known as a Silk due to the material of the gown worn, and is appointed upon their own application, supported by references. About ten per cent of the Bar are QCs. If appointed on the Lord Chancellor's recommendation to the Queen, you are eligible to appear in any legal aid case where a Judge in charge thinks it is of sufficient seriousness (I summarise) to warrant senior representation. The rates of pay are higher. Additionally, a QC can appear either pro bono or as a gun for hire in any case, agreeing the fee with his professional (solicitor) client or with his lay client through a scheme imaginatively called 'Direct Access.'

The appointment system, like any, is flawed. Outstanding candidates may be overlooked, whilst indifferent ones get the nod.

It is true the old system under which I was appointed had weaknesses. The form dealt in general terms such as, 'Are you a thoroughly good egg/bad egg?' 'Do the Judges you have appeared in front of like you/not like you?' 'Do they think you are a complete waste of space/an incomplete waste of space?'

But these days the referee is required to fill in a form referring not to the applicant's 'competence' but to 'competencies'. Who speaks like that? When in the real world have you ever spoken of someone's competencies? Does a worker get hauled before his boss for his lack of competencies? So we – the referees – end up being judged by our competency in filling in the form. Most of us are 'incompetency'.

My application was much simpler and neither of the above. A good friend of mine, Craig Rush, got drunk at a Bar Mess dinner, put his head in a well-known Lord Justice of Appeal's lap and slurred, 'Go on, make Nige a Silk.' It worked. Had he thrown up in his lap it probably would not have.

Many Silks' websites tell you that they are the best briefs of all time. I know at least twenty-seven 'best criminal barristers in the world', and I seem to recall that, according to my website, I was one of them.

The English Bar notionally adheres to the cab rank principle: any barrister with his 'For hire' sign illuminated has to take any case that flags him down. Does that mean we must represent those charged with any abomination, however close to home it strikes? Not in my view. We are not automatons. One of the Junior Counsel with whom I shared chambers was offered a brief representing one of the more recently captured Nazis. He asked me, in theory, would I take the case? (I make it clear I was never up for consideration, but would have found the choice simple.)

I said, 'No.'

'But,' he said, 'you'd represent a rapist.'

'Yes,' I said, 'but not if they raped my grandma.'

My only regret about that episode was that when one day I heard that the Defendant was visiting chambers, I did not go and kick him downstairs.

22.

Top of the pops

I must confess I have not been involved in the greatest cases in history. A bit like pretending you're on *Desert Island Discs*, I've drawn up a list of my favourite cases ever. This is it:

'Straight in at No. 1':

SOLOMON AND THE BABY, 3000 BCE (ISH)

Solomon, the wise, former King of Israel (not to be confused with Tyson Fury, presently King of the Gypsies), had to adjudicate between two mothers, each claiming that a baby belonged to them. Solomon answered their claims by saying that he would cut the baby in half (in Essex known as a 'bit of a result'). At the threat of killing the baby, one of the women spoke up, saying, 'Give it to the other.' Solomon recognised her as the true parent and gave her the baby.

Whole case probably took one hour. Fees not big.

'At No. 2 for the last 1,986 years':

EASTER TIDINGS

34 CE was an odd case. Two Defendants charged with different offences. Jesus Christ, a righteous Jew and Rabbi, whom a whole religion claims was the Messiah and certainly a good deal more than just a very naughty boy, was brought before Pontius Pilate, charged with blasphemy. Barabbas also came before him charged with theft. I am not sure it is told what he stole, but it was probably hummus. Ultimately, the Jury – the governor (Pilate) – convicted them both, but Pilate only asked that one be punished. Sadly, the man who did not steal hummus but was the Saviour of the World, was crucified.

'At No. 3':

CHARLIE IS MY DARLING, 1649

Charles I, having lost the Civil War, was brought before the Courts. He neither recognised the Court's jurisdiction nor had counsel, thus inspiring the Law Society's strap line: 'Don't lose your head, get representation now.'

'In at No. 4':

DON'T YOU HATE HIM, BABY? 1960

Adolf Eichmann was one of those who had implemented the Holocaust. Having kidnapped him from Buenos Aires, it is not apocryphal that the Israelis on the plane back promised, 'You will receive the fairest trial possible and then we will hang you.' The Eichmann trial was a jurisprudential anachronism, because whilst trying a monster, the concepts that were raised were unique. For instance, the country trying him had not been founded at the time of the crime. Equally, whilst more than six million Jews, gays and gypsies were annihilated, they were not Israelis, so how could they try him? However, the basis of universal right to try crimes (and for a state to claim jurisprudence based on the strong nexus between state and crime) made the trial not only lawful but also a milestone.

Eichmann did receive a fair trial. Then he was hanged.

The state's revulsion meant they dispersed his ashes in the sea and beyond the national limits.

I admit I have read very few legal judgements – the other one concerning an alsatian dog – but this, undoubtedly, as the foundation of many international law concepts, was the more interesting.

The Eichmann trial must have its special place in my life and this book. Equally of interest might be the controversial expression coined by Hannah Arendt and used as the title of her book, 'the banality of evil', a phrase with which – as so many did at the time of her writing – I wholeheartedly take issue.

23.

Fair is foul

Having given you my list of history's truly great trials, the rest merge into the normal diet of a Silk. I did my fair share and quite frequently more than my fair share.

So now we are moving towards the upper end of my criminal career at the Bar but, don't panic, the book has a way to go and I promise you will get your money's worth, trusting that you have paid for it.

I never stopped taking legal aid cases and, with private work in between it was a diet of murder and serious fraud, and it became non-stop. The particulars seemed to get worse and worse.

And with a whole compendium of horrific cases to my name, perhaps it's not surprising I was becoming a cynic. Who wouldn't?

The cases referred to hereafter simply raise the question, 'How can people behave like this?' Or, from a Judge's point of view, the question, 'How can a Judge remain unaffected and impartial when confronted with individuals such as these?'

As in *Macbeth*, what happens in court is often the reversal of universal norms. Fathers kill children, wives kill husbands, carers steal the life savings of their charges until, in the end, you believe you are living in a madhouse and you can believe nothing about the innate decency of people. And a Judge watches all of this unfold before him.

During the initial coronavirus lockdown, were the people who volunteered to help in hospitals and run round supplies in our communities the same as those pushing people aside to get their extra toilet paper in the Tesco queue? Do we simply have people of differing degrees of kindness, from good at the top to low lifes at the bottom – and the evil somewhere beneath that?

Or are we all capable of performing the whole gamut of acts from saintly goodness to demonic wickedness?

PART 5

Murder and mayhem

24.

Jelly beans

As with jelly beans, Defendants come in all shapes and sizes, friendly giants to unfriendly monsters – and often a mix of both.

In one case, D (as we refer to the Defendant) was just generally disturbing. He was caught by a sentencing anomaly. My solicitor instructed me to represent a man on the face of it a fair way down the list of public enemies. He was charged with attacking a woman as she passed by with her baby in a pram, slashing at her and injuring her with a knife. Serious injury, but not really serious; i.e. not Grievous Bodily Harm (GBH) with intent, but the lesser crime of Actual Bodily Harm.

I prepared to meet him in the cells at Chelmsford and my solicitor and friend Russell Haldane had warned me that I might think him, let us just say, 'unusual'. When I went into the cell he seemed to me to be fairly withdrawn, but in the words of Tom Jones, 'not unusual'. I recall that, like the rest of him, his lips were very thin. We began to discuss the case and got onto fairly difficult territory as we considered what his plea might be. As the evidence indicated, there was no doubt it was him. I could not see him escaping conviction. I sensed he was resisting my advice from the way he began to rhythmically rock back and forth in his chair. I was reminded of Anthony Perkins in *Psycho*, impersonating his dead mother in the attic of the Bates Motel (Sorry. I should have warned 'spoiler alert'.) My slight anxiety became less slight as one sleeve of his jumper rode up, revealing slash marks on his arm. He fixed me with a stare. I moved slowly toward the cell door. As it happens, assault is rare between counsel and clients. It is recognised that if I was not there – defending or prosecuting – some other sap would be.

Upon his guilty plea the Defendant became an anachronism, caught in the vortex of a sentencing nightmare. Although the current offence was not of the worst kind, he had a previous 'qualifying' serious offence that made him eligible for – and, eventually, in receipt of – a sentence of Imprisonment for Public Protection (IPP). An IPP was a novel invention of Parliament that made him subject to release not based on his good behaviour but subject to the discretion/whim of the Home Office. But when would that be? Ultimately, these sentences gained disapproval as people found themselves incarcerated for disproportionately long times or – as it was otherwise known – ever.

Among the variety of Defendants, step up: the 'D. Brothers'.

Into the horror league came brothers at the time regarded as two of the most dangerous men in England. Old-fashioned armed robbers being chased down by the Flying Squad. Massive men both. One of the things I have not conveyed so far is that such people often have a charm of their own, and are very easy to represent. Thus it was with my client. He was cornered on a riverbank by the Flying Squad with weapons drawn. He pleaded with the officer, 'Put one in my back – I can't do eighteen years,' which ultimately assisted the Judge with his sentencing.

It all got rather messy when it dawned on my client that his brother had grassed him up to the police. Until then they had both sat impassively in the dock at the back of Chelmsford Crown Court. As the penny dropped, my fellow grabbed his brother by the shirt and moved him back toward the stairs going down to the cells. Like the Red Sea, the dock officers parted, leaving a gap through which he threw his brother downstairs and smashed his head into some reinforced glass. You could hear the fight in all of the adjoining courts in all of the neighbouring counties.

In that case, I led one of my close friends, Mike Epstein. He was not long out of pupillage, and this was a rather daunting case with a rather daunting client. Having made my closing speech to the Jury, I was due to go and start my next case in Norwich and left. We were at the end of the case, where a surgeon might pull off his gloves, saying, 'Close up, will you?'

Within an hour of arriving in Norwich my phone rang. It was Mike. 'I've got a problem ...' I couldn't believe that within two hours an issue had arisen which he couldn't deal with, and so very intemperately, I cut him off. 'I'm having my fxxking lunch ...' Click. Later, we sorted the problem, but forever after, calls between us usually began with him saying, 'If you're not having your fxxking lunch ...'

That wasn't the last thing that arose of note in that case. There being a thirty-second gap in my practice, I had begun to represent the prosecution in a theft case against a man who had stolen the life savings of an old-age pensioner, having wheedled his way into her house. She kept the money in a bread bin that the thief had found.

I had gone down to chew the fat with my client, the robber brother, whilst waiting for the next case to start. He began: 'Oh, Mr Lifman [remember they had abolished 'th' in Essex many years previously], you're prosecuting that scumbag that stole the old lady's savings, aren't you? I wouldn't trouble yourself, if I were you, we're going to sort that one out down here ...'

What took place that day was rough justice. Very rough justice.

25.

A little knowledge

A little knowledge is said to be a bad thing. Personally, I find it all counts, especially if it is not knocking around in great abundance. Defendants pretrial, particularly if banged up in prison, have little better to do than study a bit of law. At their fingertips they have the lawyers' criminal bible, *Archbold*, known in prison as 'Archibold'. And just as Andy Dufresne was a barrack room accountant in *Shawshank Redemption*, there are generally no shortages of backroom lawyers – both actual and faux – in jail.

The buzzword and worst nightmare for a Defendant used to be a charge of conspiracy. Actually, conspiracy was generally nothing to be afeared. Whereas 'theft', 'robbery' and 'GBH' generally mean what they say, conspiracy just means the agreement to do it, that is the crime. But there is no such crime as simple conspiracy. It is conspiracy to *do* something, e.g. to steal, to rob, to do GBH. Thus, 'conspiracy to do GBH' means agreeing to cause someone really serious harm. The circumstances of involvement in an agreement to commit a crime may change from person to person. For example, how long were you involved? Did you think better of it and drop out? Was your involvement to be very much subsidiary to others? All could mean you attract a lesser sentence than the actual shooters, stabbers or other conspirators.

But to an uninformed Defendant their fear arose from three ideas: the belief that conspiracy itself, attached to no specific offence but just generally, was a crime; that it carries a maximum of life imprisonment; that, because of the breadth of its nature, a Jury would be bound to convict of it.

Whilst no. 2 is true, 1 and 3 are not, and as many acquittals arise where conspiracy to do something is charged as in any other case. But their fear was not to be assuaged.

That buzzword was joined by two other buzzwords: 'joint enterprise'. Again, the belief was that there was a crime called 'joint enterprise' rather than the actual situation. One cannot be guilty of joint enterprise, but only of a particular crime *by virtue* of joint enterprise. This means a getaway driver in a robbery is part of a joint enterprise and equally as guilty as the stick-up man. The crime, however, is robbery. Throughout crime, the two central issues are the act (what happened) and the mental element (were you aware it was going to happen and intended it to happen?).

An example of the application of the principles of joint enterprise that frequented my practice, was as follows: in the midlands an Asian family was targeted.

A home was fire-bombed and an aged husband and wife tragically killed. Four people were accused of driving to the street seeking 'revenge' in the form of an 'honour killing'. A young girl had had the temerity to elope with a man she loved, forsaking the man she did not. The men came up with firebombs. They parked around the corner and two left the car on foot to deliver them. They chose the wrong house. The elderly people within it were wholly unrelated to the episode. The defence of the two in the car was that they did not know what was going on. They believed the men who left the car did so to go and 'score' some drugs and that is why they had driven for two and a half hours.

Whether they were charged with conspiracy to murder or joint enterprise murder, the main principles were the same: if the two in the car had accompanied the others as knowing parties to the crime of murder intending to cause at least serious harm, they were guilty. If not, not. But it was a tough crime to hear about and remain perfectly neutral.

Where is all this leading, I hear you ask? It is to the reality that it is exceptionally difficult for Judges hearing these cases day in, day out, to remain dispassionate about their general views of the guilt or innocence of those coming before them. They are mere mortals, not robots. For a number of Judges this is their daily diet. As one nightmare ends, the next horror story begins. And it is the same for the advocates.

They come to anticipate that their next client or Defendant will be a clone of the last one, a cycle that repeats itself throughout their careers. What does this do for their view of Defendants, never mind humanity? How objective and dispassionate can their views be?

26.

Relatively speaking

These are some of the cases in which I appeared where normality was turned on its head.

SONS KILLING FATHERS

A client murdered his father by setting fire to him in circumstances that would be fascinating were they not so dire. The son suffered from enormous mental health issues, and fate chose to compound his difficulties. He was an epileptic subject to the most extreme of seizures, which were beyond his coping. And so it was decided to try out a new drug on him. The effect was remarkable – and not in a good way. The drug turned what were fits for all the world to see into fits being acted out in his brain. The phenomenon was known as forced normalisation. The effect was to make him suffer an earthquake inside his head. Thus, rather than on the floor, he writhed internally.

Whilst undergoing such a seizure he killed his father in his bed and set fire to him. If the acts were beyond his control, the correct verdict was manslaughter and the sentence far less than was attracted by cases of murder with intent to kill or cause really serious harm. That was the outcome. Whilst one unimaginative prosecutor wished to try him for murder, when he became unavailable, his successor took the more compassionate course.

The Bar can generally distinguish what feels like a murder case and what feels like a manslaughter case.

FATHERS KILLING DAUGHTERS

A man repaired to his attic and used his necktie to strangle his two very young and very sweet daughters. He then attempted to commit suicide by taking rat poison. This was ineffective and he was discovered, several days later, in the attic with them. The suggestion of diminished responsibility did not carry water, and he was convicted of murder.

SIBLING RIVALRY

A case of sibling rivalry took me to the provinces to represent a stepbrother of a guy whom the (step) brother and another had murdered and buried in the forest. There had been a falling out, and in true *Godfather* style, they had assured him he would be OK whilst their mother was alive. Within weeks of her death, they had told the victim they all had to meet in a forest in Sussex to sort out the will. Clearly, the victim thought there must be a solicitor's office in the middle of a forest. There they met, stabbed him to death and decapitated him. We heard how quicklime was poured on the separated head and body, but they had buried the head just feet away from the torso. What was the point? Both would be found within minutes of each other.

What was the point of any of this? At least a body was found, even if not in one piece. In other cases, some tried their luck in getting rid of a body that was never found again.

Life is always a learning curve, and one came to learn from a very effective 'Missing Body Team'. They unearth all of the latest financial profile or the lack of it and put together all of the features that indicate the person is not coming back. Mind you, the swathes of dried blood beneath the lino in the bathroom, as well as the ordering and replacement of the living room carpet, was added support for the idea that the victim had tired of his current address.

I suppose the reversal of the usual loving role of mother and son can seem the most heinous, but you might take that with a pinch of salt. Indeed, death was occasioned by more than a pinch of salt.

I told you how my top cop, Dick, had become a solicitor and sent me the most interesting case. Now's the time to consider it.

Forgive the fact that humour will now take a short cigarette break.

27.

A pinch of salt

Mrs X had two children. Whilst one developed normally the second faced a constant series of debilitating illnesses plus an overwhelming lethargy. The child was going downhill rapidly.

He was admitted to two hospitals, the first one local to the mother's area, where he did not improve, and thence to a hospital of national repute. There he fared little better, coupled with which the blood and urine samples that were taken from him for testing demonstrated a strange quality. His mother came to see him daily and sat the lonely vigil of a mother at her wits' end.

After a number of weeks without improvement, the national hospital changed its tack. Instead of focusing on the child they made the nurses keep their focus on the mother. They believed the samples that were being supplied from the bedside were hers and not the child's. The ratio of nurses in attendance was 2:1. Still nothing was spotted. But then came a development. A Registrar who was taking a strong interest in the case came up with the idea that the child was suffering from a condition known as encephalitis lethargica, a syndrome recognised after World War I amongst veterans who became and remained weak and disengaged for long periods of time.

Mrs X was delighted. At last, here was a diagnosis, and where there is a diagnosis, surely a cure cannot be far behind. Sadly, it did not work like that, and no cure was forthcoming. Instead came a new revelation. A blood sample, purporting to have been taken from the child, was found to contain menstrual blood. Yet Mrs X was always under surveillance. The expression Munchausen Syndrome by Proxy began to be bandied around. Was Mum harming the child?

The staff had one more card to play. Admission of the child to the psychiatric unit would help them watch the child, keep Mum at bay and explore a psychological explanation for the sickness. But worse was to come. The toxic nature of relatively small amounts of salt is well-documented. The child was found having ingested a great deal of salt, and died.

The mother was charged with murder.

Occasionally the law steps in and delivers an unexpected gift. Christmas arrives early. The 'gift' was that there had been hearings in the family court after the son had died. The court was trying to decide where the living child was better off, with the mother or father. The Family Court decided with the father upon the basis that, 'upon the balance of probabilities', the mother had killed the other child. However, the Judge went on to say that he could not be sure 'beyond a reasonable doubt' that she had killed him or with the intention required for murder (killing or causing really serious harm). It was a pupil who dug out a legal principle referred to as the 'Hunter principle'. This stated that one tribunal might bind another, as it might mean that the mother could not be tried for murder. I leapt on it with uncharacteristic enthusiasm; like a lion on an impala is probably overstating it, but I wouldn't let it go. Our trial Judge (who also prosecuted the case I refer to later in 'Palm tree justice') accepted the principle and ruled that the mother could only be tried for manslaughter.

Before the trial I went with my Junior, Adam Budworth, to see a paediatrician in Manchester to try and get some expert help in what had been going on here. After an hour or so going around the houses, our good doctor pronounced his view. It was hostile to our client's interests. We were not offending any professional rules by not using him in the trial, but clearly it would be pointless.

We were left with two avenues to assist us in understanding the medicalese, by consulting with either a medical relative (it's handy when your brother-in-law 'Dr Ed' is a consultant paediatrician) or one of Adam's friends, Dr Google. We used both. Adam consulted with his friend each night, arriving in the morning newly qualified in another speciality. Nephrology, cardiology – you name it, Adam learned all about it in one night. Dr Google had the lot.

The trial was fascinating. The Crown's case was that the child had no discernable definable illness, the samples provided were tampered with by the mother and, as she was the only realistic candidate, she must have killed him. The defence relied on the suggestion (supported by a Registrar) that he was suffering from a true illness and that someone else inserted salt into his drip – the likely candidate being a rogue nurse. Over many weeks, the court heard evidence from over fifty witnesses, gleaned from the medical fraternity of both hospitals where the child had stayed, one arguably being the world's leading children's hospital. They traced the history of the boy's treatment at each hospital and the bafflement of the staff. We fought to try and show that he was truly ill, which, of course, he was. What caused it remained a mystery.

Like all remarkable tales, two twists remained.

The first was that a packet of salt *was* found in a nurse's locker. It followed that if the child's illness was real, a rogue nurse might have killed him. But secondly came the revelation that the mother had self-harmed seriously as a child, and it was this that the Jury clearly found unlocked the puzzle. The lady sadly suffered Munchausen Syndrome by Proxy. The Jury determined that it was she who was tampering with her child's samples to ensure he would be at the forefront of the attention of doctors and, in frustration, had administered salt poison; and it was she who had put the box of salt in the nurse's locker.

The Jury found her guilty of manslaughter, but her sentence from the Judge reflected real compassion for her confused mental state.

28.

The worst of the worst

As with Defendants, the crimes themselves come in all different shapes and sizes. Judges are in fact well known for rarely if ever imposing the most severe sentence the law allows. There will always be somebody whose behaviour is worse. But not in the case of O.

I was instructed to represent a gentleman named O. Obviously there are other letters to his name which, if of any interest, you will find in the Notes at the end of this book. For reasons best known to himself, he decided to ignore the option of counselling and instead attended his partner's house with a sawn-off shotgun, along with another gun, a rope, an axe and petrol. It combined the best of Cluedo and Mousetrap. Trouble is it was not a game. He shot his partner and, in what remains the worst image I've seen in my life, he put his two-year-old child against a bannister and shot her. In death, she looked like a porcelain doll.

O received the rare distinction of a whole-life sentence, meaning he would die in prison with no chance of parole. The validity of this was questioned in the Court of Appeal, who tested whether it was consistent with European jurisprudence. They believed it was, and O returned to his cell.

The haunting picture of his doll-like daughter was juxtaposed with Mr O's own image. At the end of the episode O had turned the gun on himself, but as his attempted suicide was less than heartfelt it merely took about a third of his face away. Again, fate took its turn. Within weeks he had died from cancer that nobody knew he had.

It is not only or always the good that die young. But how can any advocate or Judge appearing in cases such as these not be affected at the deepest of levels? How can they look the world squarely in the face and love their fellow man?

PART 6

Pick'n'mix

29.

My health, your safety

Not all crimes have the same general reputation. Two categories can appear closer to civil offences rather than criminal ones. Let's look briefly at them.

OLD BOILERS

As we move down the compendium of Defendants we reach two areas of law, still criminal in nature but usually associated with the less reprehensible of our criminal fraternity. Often serious but occupying a world where guns don't tend to be toted nor blood spilt. The worlds of health and safety offences and white-collar crime, i.e. fraud.

If the coronavirus taught us nothing else it is that problems arise only too readily when you're living at home with an old boiler. I'm referring of course to your Combie.

It was faulty boilers that comprised a lot of my health and safety practice.

Health and safety cases are generally referred to as HSE cases, after the Health and Safety Executive that prosecute them. They are usually upsetting, needless, avoidable tragedies. The typical scenario is one where the boiler is serviced and the servicer proclaims your boiler is unsafe and may well be emitting carbon monoxide. He tells you that the law demands he shut it down.

The householder's response is always the same. 'You can't shut it down. There are of four us and a dog. We need heat and hot water to bath.'

Eventually, nagged into submission, the servicer says, 'All right, get a device from Ryman that tells you when the CO levels are unacceptable, keep the windows open and I'll be back tomorrow. Don't bath the dog.'

Tomorrow, when he returns, the only one left is the dog. The fatalities that arise lead to HSE prosecutions for manslaughter and/or breaches of regulations involving failing to undertake a proper risk assessment and/or to properly guard against the risk.

'What do I know about old boilers ... nothing, but I know a man that does.'

It so happens that two of my former pupils became leading exponents in health and safety law and, as the saying goes, but in this case literally, 'wrote the book'. One, Jim Ageros, about whom more later, and the other, Richard Matthews. Both became QCs.

In fact, the cases are not rocket science, although ironically if rocket science went wrong, that too would be dealt with by the HSE.

The boiler cases can involve the reckless behaviour of the householders. I recall one particular plumber who had bowed down to the pressure of the homeowner. As in the above scenario, having found the boiler leaking CO, he was persuaded to provide the 'Ryman's gadget, window open' advice.

The dog was fine but the human occupants died. The plumber pleaded guilty to a regulatory charge and the HSE, rather fortunately for him, dropped the manslaughter allegation. The plumber was over the moon that he was only fined. Naturally, I chose my moment to strike. I asked him if he had time to service my boiler. After all, lightning never strikes twice, does it? He did it perfectly well, and anyway I bought a CO alarm from Ryman and haven't closed the window or bathed the dog since.

IT FELL OF THE BACK OF A LORRY

We pass by Hiabs every day. These are the cranes on the back of a lorry. They are effectively a machine on a machine. It's a straightforward bit of kit. The lorry parks up and the crane swings out to work from the back. Stabilisers are put out to stop the lorry toppling over, as the crane hangs out over one side. The Hiab operates independently of the lorry.

Sorry, did I say the stabilisers are put out? Not on this day in Suffolk they weren't.

The driver failed to put the stabilisers out and the lorry toppled over, killing someone. A Jury had little sympathy and the driver ended up with a short time in custody.

You know how, when we are dealing with something, the world seems to be full of it? This always happens with cases. I did a trial about stolen scaffolding poles. I don't know if it's still the custom, but firms used to paint the ends of their poles their own colour, each firm using a different colour. If it's pink, it must belong to Poles Apart, if it's blue it must be Girders Incorporated. The trial concerned Poles Apart stealing and painting over Girders Inc. Wherever I went the world was full of poles, and now the same with Hiabs. I refused to start the day's business before my Junior, and I had driven around and spotted a Hiab. He must have thought me exceptionally superstitious, or just bonkers.

TAKING THE BLAME

Finally, on the HSE front, a most unusual case. I was asked to advise on a gas explosion that took place in a village where a charitable trust ran a group of houses for the less fortunate. There had been a gas explosion, killing an elderly couple.

The trust was a voluntary organisation of people freely and generously giving of their time. However, if there was to be a prosecution, it would have to be a member of the trust prosecuted on behalf of all of them. They were allowed to select their own fall guy/s.

The trust very shrewdly nominated two members who were pillars of society, telling the HSE if you are going to prosecute anyone choose one of these two gentlemen. It was a bit like the 'I'm Spartacus' scene, but two of them pronouncing it at the same time:

'I'm a trust member, prosecute me.' 'No, I'm a trust member...' and so on.

However, rather than Kirk Douglas, the trust put up a retired general in his late seventies and an eighty-four-year-old gentleman with cancer as the candidates to prosecute.

The HSE was in a cleft stick. If no prosecution was brought it would appear as if people were being let off the hook because of their elitist position. Equally, if they were prosecuted, it would seem as if people in truth blameless for the explosion were being penalised for giving freely of their time and running this village. So who would come forward in future and do this sort of voluntary work?

The Attorney General, Lord Goldsmith, asked to see a representative from the prosecution. As I was on holiday, I asked Jim if he would go. I said, 'Tell him you are here as Nigel Lithman is on holiday, but he sends his regards. That should do the trick ... huh?'

Lord Goldsmith reacted exactly as a man in high office should. 'Never mind about all that, what the hell's going on here? Why are we prosecuting two old men, one who is a general and the other who has cancer, who have nothing whatever to do with this explosion?'

Jim is a man who can spot the way the wind is blowing. The astute Junior observed that the senior law officer in Her Majesty's government had taken a view, and with those words, the Gordian Knot was cut and the prosecution fell.

30.

Fraud – other people's greed

I suppose many might find it strange that, overall, I have always preferred blood and guts to white-collar crime, albeit I have spent enough of my life immersed in telephone schedules and bank statements.

In many ways, I was suited to an old-fashioned QC's life, which means whilst others waded through the source material, line by line, I was to be found paddling or strolling in the base hills of the information. Like most people I remember where I was at the time the planes flew into the Twin Towers in New York on 9/11. (I, of course, can also remember where I was when J.F.K. was murdered, though I resent the wag who says I can probably recall the assassination of Archduke Franz Ferdinand that triggered World War I.) When the planes struck the towers, I was being instructed by solicitor Samantha Leonard and was prosecuted by Dame Linda Dobbs, as now is, in Inner London Crown Court.

I remember the Judge turning to my team and saying, 'Mr Lithman, I would like some help with the detail concerning a particular motor vehicle. Please don't think me discourteous, but I think it's probably a question better directed to your Junior.' In other words, I could better deal with the broad-brush details, and by broad, I mean the sort of brush that could do two walls and a ceiling, both coats, in twenty minutes.

As with all my other work, some cases that stand out do so for their fun. They were in the Midlands.

THE OSTRICH THAT LAID THE GOLDEN EGG

The ostrich farm had all of the ingredients that constitute a fraud. Those are, an item that can be called the subject matter of the fraud, a false representation, a number of duped individuals and a television newsreader.

X and Y offered for investment ostriches being bred on a farm in the Midlands. A number were brought over from South Africa. You could invest in their rearing at different rates. You could invest in an 'old bird' or a 'young chick'. It was a very different era. Now try repeating that for six weeks during the trial and not laughing. I did not go quietly. You must have worked out by now I am a giggler.

Fraudsters get lazy. First, you were investing in birds, then in eggs and then in microchips representing unborn ostriches.

So to 'old birds and 'young chicks' you could now add 'eggs' and 'chips'. Of course, you can sell the same item and the same ostrich many times over. And the fraudsters did – fraud is the only business where 100 per cent of something is nowhere near enough. In this case, it was the investors, not the ostriches, that buried their heads in the sand as to what was actually going on.

The Defence, as so often was: 'You have jumped to the wrong conclusion. It is not fraud, but a wholly legitimate enterprise based on a sound investment. The birds exist: both old birds and young chicks; we misrepresented nothing; the investment is AAA. Plus, ostrich meat is the new elixir of life; meat high in good stuff, low in bad stuff (if you can understand the science). So we present you with a perfect opportunity to invest all you have and for us to steal your money which will ruin you, but for our part we agree to go to jail.'

And that's how it all panned out. I mentioned that you also need a 'celebrity' to get involved in the fraud as an investor. This is usually a newsreader or someone who has been on 'I'm Hardly a Celebrity but Get Me Outta Here'. The trial process allows for either the witness to be summonsed to be questioned, or their evidence read as agreed. Invariably, the 'celebrity' will be summonsed.

'Yes,' says the Judge. 'Any questions, Mr Lithman?'

'Not really, Your Honour, I was just interested to see what she looked like when she wasn't reading the news.'

31.

Horses for courses

I was going to say Peter W. was larger than life. But, really, the entry fee for appearing in this book is being larger than life. The fraud that was alleged against Peter W. – and, six weeks later, was deemed by a Jury to be the fraud he committed – was much closer to the traditional Ponzi scheme. However, this was not robbing Peter to pay Paul, but was Peter robbing absolutely everybody to pay Peter.

The vehicle of the fraud were two companies offering rates too good to be true. Because they were. The proceeds of the fraud amongst other things were put towards the purchase of a racehorse. So it could hardly be claimed that he wasted it. It wasn't that Peter spoke nonsense, it was the way he spoke nonsense. He had a pronounced stutter and a pair of glasses that he could peer over as he did so. He used them both to good effect as he would set out to explain the inexplicable. I would end every court session in hysterics. Fortunately, there was a vestibule into the barristers' robing room where I could lie down with my legs in the air, laughing. I appeared to resemble a bluebottle on the windowsill in its death throes. To the rest of the Bar, they just attributed it to the fact that the case was in Nottingham and I was from London. The effects on my Junior, Richard Matthews, were much the same.

At one stage Peter W. appeared to get bored of the proceedings and, before we had started the day, he jumped up, announcing: 'I'm off, tell the Judge I'll write.'

I duly went into court and thoroughly enjoyed making the most ridiculous observation ever made to a Judge: 'I'm sorry, Your Honour, the Defendant has gone – but he says he'll write.'

Another moment in the trial really beggared belief. Our prosecutor was Peter Benson, later to become a Judge. He occupied the same place each morning in the robing room, sitting at a table, smoking a small cigar and reading the *Racing Post*. Like the Defendant, he was a racing man to his fingertips.

The moment arose in this way. Peter the Prosecutor had traced the fact that Peter the Defendant's horse had been running at Southall on a Bank Holiday Monday, and before the weekend, Peter the Defendant had cleared a substantial swathe of cash from the company accounts.

'You did that, Mr W., in order to bet on your horse on the Monday, didn't you?' suggested Peter the Prosecutor.

'Come on, Mr Benson,' said Peter the Defendant. 'You can do better than that. You're a racing man, did you bet on my horse that day?'

Credit to Peter the Prosecutor, as he was happy to have an exchange with a fellow punter. 'No, Mr W., I did not.'

Peter W. jumped in. 'No, Mr Benson, you did not because the horse was no bloody good – so nor did I. I did not take out money from the company accounts to fritter away.' After a very theatrical pause, Peter the Defendant added, 'But I'll tell you one thing you don't know. Do you know who finished last in the second race that day?'

'No,' said Peter the Prosecutor, 'I don't.'

By now, the Judge and Jury were sitting up, aghast at this conversation that might as well have been taking place in a local William Hill Turf Accountants.

'Well, look it up overnight and we'll mention it tomorrow,' demanded Peter the Defendant, who liked nothing more than to take control of the proceedings.

The next day we resumed at 10.30 with Peter back in the witness box. 'Well,' asked Peter the Defendant, 'did you look up who finished last in the second race that day?'

Peter the Prosecutor, with a very broad smile, answered, 'The horse that finished last in the second race was called "Mr Benson".'

The whole court laughed; we were flabbergasted. No word of a lie. What were the chances? The same chances as the delightful Peter W. being acquitted. Probably 1,000–1.

32.

Morality tales

I spoke before a bit glibly about lack of moral fibre, but whilst Judges often say, 'This is a court of law, not morals', and whilst that means we don't censure infidelity if irrelevant to the case we are trying, some cases do have morals at their heart, and may involve moral norms being turned on their head.

WHITE-COLLAR CRIME (WITH THE COLLARS TURNED AROUND)

Such an obvious group I was asked to represent were men of the cloth. A Catholic archbishop came to see me and asked if I would take cases representing Catholic priests charged with indecency against children. What was envisaged was my moving from court to court, representing this holy sea of priests. I said I would, provided the Church had no issue with the fact that I was Jewish. They said they did not.

The first case was representing a priest in Birmingham who had insinuated his way into a family's home. The tale became a blueprint for others. The child attended a Catholic school. The priest would attend the family home where he was literally venerated. He secured the unthinking approval of the parents to take their son out for the day and then on school trips, during which he seriously abused him.

Before that he was a regular visitor to the home. The deceit would arise because even as the parents came into a living room and caught the priest touching their child, as happened on one occasion in this case, they simply did not believe their eyes, such was the esteem in which the family held him.

He gave evidence that the family had lied. The evidence was overwhelming. The idea that a priest was prepared to lie on oath was spellbinding.

Before the trial he asked, 'Do you think the Jury would be biased against me on the basis that I'm a Catholic priest charged with abuse?'

I answered: 'Well, put it this way, I have told a number of friends that I am currently representing a Catholic priest, and none of them have asked me what for.'

Interestingly, he did not ask me if *I* would be prejudiced against him.

Despite the best efforts of my excellent Junior, Valerie Charbit, and I, he was convicted. The reality is that we were professionals, doing our job, and it did not occur to either of us to do anything but our best. But the notion of a man of G-d taking the Bible and lying on it is really rather terrifying.

ROAD KILL

I was also approached by the Campaign Against Drink Driving (CADD) to see if I would take on their private prosecutions. These were cases where drivers, when drunk, had collided with and killed a road user. The fact that this group and the Archbishop would approach me was ironic in a way, as I was neither a Catholic nor teetotal. The deaths on the road were cases where the Crown Prosecution Service (CPS) had formed a view that the law of causing death by reckless driving should be rarely used, as there but for the grace of G-d went we all. The consequences of the driving were largely deemed irrelevant. This, of course, was nonsense. An essential feature, if not *the* essential feature, was the death occasioned. Whilst I could be brought in to bring the prosecution on behalf of CADD, the CPS were enabled to take over a case and drop it, which, nine times out of ten, they did.

The insurance I took out was that when the case was sent to trial from the Magistrates Court, I would announce to the Magistrates that, if the CPS intended to take over and drop a case, it would be a travesty of justice. This was designed to embarrass them into continuing the prosecutions and not dropping them. This usually worked, and hence families would find solace in the fact that drivers who had killed their loved ones were brought to trial.

I know that not everyone is George Washington, but if you are a priest who has abused a child or a driver who has perhaps killed one, is there not an overwhelming urge to tell the truth and try and put the record straight?

Perhaps I am not allowing sufficiently for shame and self-delusion.

33.

Palm tree justice

The Bar is not just a place of angst. Occasionally – oh, joy – it all comes together.

I can honestly say I've not only been to all courts north and south of Chelmsford, but I also stepped forth on a case in the 1980s on the island of Diego Garcia. Diego is a part of the British Indian Ocean Territory. It is owned by the UK but leased to the Americans, who used it as an airbase. It was from there that they launched Operation Desert Storm, the first Gulf war of 1991.

The island is the closest thing to heaven on Earth. If you have been good on Earth you will go there when you die, whereas if you have been wicked you will go to Rochdale. It has the unrivalled beaches of the Indian Ocean – Diego Garcia, that is, not Rochdale. The only occupants apart from US soldiers are a handful of Brits, including the Commander of the Island, and the only rule amongst the soldiers is that there should be no married couples, as this was thought to promote unhealthy rivalries.

As a result, every soldier had forty-two partners.

My clerk, John Grimmer, was contacted by a solicitor of whom both of us were very fond. Ralph

Haeems had been solicitor to the Kray twins, of East End gangland fame. Ralph had been approached by a friend who was patron to the United Seamen's Service of the USA. One of their members had got into trouble for a serious assault upon a soldier. And now, as usual, fate conspired to make its own destiny and, on this occasion, my good fortune.

There had been a murder on the island, and a Prosecutor was going to prosecute both cases. Someone was coming from Hong Kong to represent him, and the Judge, Sir John Spry, was coming from another British territory to try him. The Foreign Office offered the seaman the same representative as the alleged murderer. He refused, saying he wanted a UK advocate. Ralph was contacted and he in turn contacted our clerk.

Ralph had asked me. 'Do you want to go on BA, first class to the Seychelles?'

I said, 'Of course.'

It didn't happen. He sent me economy to Diego Garcia on Pakistan International Airways with his assistant, Martin Lee. But it was via a stopover in Singapore, and was marvellous. It was Palm Tree Heaven administering Palm Tree Justice. My stay was extended in Heaven due to the misfortune of Sir John Spry having a heart attack on the way over. My heart went out to Sir John (who knows, it might have helped), and I just hoped he got some pleasure in knowing he had extended my stay in paradise by six weeks. Everything was delayed.

Upon his arrival, I went and discussed sentence with him in his quarters over a cocktail. He first asked me if I had been called to the Bar in the British Indian Ocean Territory. In other words, was I qualified and entitled to represent someone as an advocate in the British Ocean Territories? I guess it might be thought that, having travelled to Singapore before getting the weekly military transporter out to Diego, I had left this matter a little late to attend to. I confessed that this 'technicality' had been overlooked.

'How do I apply?' I asked. He replied that I had to apply to him. I said, 'OK, I'm applying.' He replied, 'OK, I'm granting.'

I put it to Sir John that, if it were not for trying the murder, my client's rather paltry little stabbing of a soldier would have been dealt with by the island's Commander and would have resulted in a mere fine. Sir John agreed he would do the same, and therefore my client would be fined. We picked a date for the hearing. I chose the day after the weekly flight departed, ensuring yet another six heavenly days yachting in the clear-blue sea and hanging out of the side of a helicopter, held on by a safety harness, feet taking the air.

We all dressed up in our court gear – wigs and gowns – and the case was heard in the Strategic Air Command building. It took forty minutes one Thursday, meaning the whole experience lasted six weeks and forty minutes.

I have always had a soft spot for Americans. They hosted my stay there. Frankly, they found their British hosts mean-spirited. One day, my American friend, Bob Stephenson, who had commanded helicopters in Vietnam, pointed to the neat strip on the side of the road. As you looked at it you realised that this closely shorn grass bordered an area that looked like it was inhabited by Tarzan and Jane.

Bob said, 'We even mow the jungle for them, and the Brits still don't like us.' The idea of a Flymo hovering over dense jungle was indeed a thought to be conjured with.

Some will have already gleaned that I am a terrible show-off. I dispute that. I truly believe that I am an excellent show-off. But there is one episode from Diego Garcia I would like to bequeath to the charity shop that will end up putting this book on the 5p shelf. I was made an officer on the island, being given a temporary rank of Major by the Americans. I must say it did seem odd when a young soldier one day came to a halt saying, 'Permission to use your beach, sir.' I gave it grudgingly, as this doubled its occupancy. But put it this way, social-distancing rules would not have created any issue that day.

Later that evening I was walking towards the officers' mess, which was under three palm trees. An American officer fell into step with me and, on the way over, we had a friendly chat. I explained what I was doing on the island, and that I was a barrister.

I added that he had probably heard of me from a number of the cases I had been in in Chelmsford. After a few minutes, I thought I'd better feign some interest in who he was. He explained he was General Colin Powell, US Chief of Staff and Commander of USS *Coral Sea*, the largest aircraft carrier in the world. I quickly put him in his place by saying, 'OK, it's not a competition.' I then went back to telling him about some of the Actual Bodily Harm cases I had been involved in.

Something similar happened on the occasion I was invited (as with all Silks and Judicial appointments) to one of the Queen's garden parties. I was chatting to a guy who said he was from the Seychelles as we headed in the direction of cucumber sandwiches (no edges). I told him about some of the work at Luton Crown Court. Again, my innate good breeding led me eventually to ask him what he did in the Seychelles. He said he was Prime Minister. Some people just can't resist showing off.

PART 7

The scales of justice

34.

The presumption of innocence

And so the years passed.

Judges looked on, as the scales carried by blind-folded Justice began tipping in the Defendants' favour. I am not saying I was for or against it. But that is certainly the way it was and, within my professional duties, I exploited the situation to benefit my clients. Lawyers themselves tend not to get involved in innocence and guilt. As Mr Jaggers said in *Great Expectations*, 'I am interested in verdicts, not innocence.' Putting it crudely, if a client says he is innocent – although everything might suggest the opposite – you will fight tooth and nail to achieve his acquittal. Largely, this involves picking holes in the prosecution case or hoping your client will be more or less as credible as those who have given evidence against him.

And there are a number of features that weight the case in his favour:

a The burden or onus of proving the case is on the prosecution. He doesn't have to prove anything.

b The prosecution must prove guilt to a high standard

– the Jury must be sure of guilt ('beyond a reasonable doubt'). He does not have to prove anything.

c As with everything else, it is easier to knock something down than build something up.

d Whilst the client might be a congenital idiot, it is possible that his counsel may not be. It is his counsel who gets to address the Jury last and persuade them that black is white and that a space traveller came down from the planet Throg to commit the deed of which the client has been accused.

e Whilst there were six members of the Birmingham Six and four members of the Guildford Four wrongly convicted, there are very many others that are wrongly acquitted – the theory being that it is better that a hundred people are wrongly acquitted than one person wrongly convicted.

f Where a client maintains his innocence, his lawyer is not supposed to second-guess him and persuade him of his guilt.

g In fact, even if he says he is guilty, he does not have to plead guilty – although you, as his lawyer, cannot be a knowing party to his misleading the court.

The lawyers reading this book (particularly the pedants in our profession, whom I reckon might number 20 per cent) will ask me to remind you that even someone who tells you he is guilty is entitled to a trial to make the prosecution prove its case. But you cannot let him give evidence to the court that you know is a lie. This can be avoided by not calling him into the witness box to tell lies on oath – indeed, not calling him to give evidence at all – and then making a speech to the Jury maintaining that the Crown cannot prove its case.

Let us just consider 'not calling your client'. At the end of the prosecution's case, it is the turn of the defence to call the Defendant and any supporting witnesses they might have to give their evidence. The Judge will warn the Defendant that the Jury may hold it against him if he decides not to go into the witness box (or take the stand, as the Yanks call it). You tell your client they most probably will hold it against him. But putting it shortly, it might be better not to call your client to give evidence than call him and let him cock it up.

What is the risk of not calling him? In law nowadays a Jury is entitled to hold that fact against him, but if counsel can persuade the Jury that there is not a solid case to answer in the first place, he might talk them out of it.

If you are confident that the Crown's case can be argued against without evidence, then it may be worth the risk in not calling him. Why? Because you can usually rely on your client to make a hash of it. Why should you think that? Well, he got caught, didn't he? So, if it's going well, why spoil it?

Let's stick with the concept of not calling your client to give evidence. This gives more tactical problems to lawyers than perhaps any other. To a Piscean like me, it led to an unmitigated fog of indecision. Many lawyers would pass the buck to the client. 'It's up to you,' they'd say. Of course it is up to them, but they deserve better than non-committal advice. Is that the best you can do? You should advise, even if the decision is the client's to make.

As was said to the man who rode a bicycle across Niagara Falls along a tightrope, it is of course a balancing act. If a Defendant chooses not to give evidence, will a Jury take the view he has something to hide? Or, even if they are not sure, will that outweigh any legal caution they are given?

35.

Across the pond

In referring to the right not to give evidence, it can do no harm to compare jurisdictions and have a quick look at life in America. There, in the celebrated cases where Defendants did not give evidence, I am left dubious about the soundness of tactics their attorneys employed.

As I've said, as a QC, I represented the English Bar as part of the team of Judges at the Florida Convention on Advocacy, along with two Juniors from the UK Bar. I had applied for the gig, which was one week in Gainesville, Florida. I flew into Orlando accompanied by the sort of electrical storm that grounded many an Apollo mission and brought Frankenstein's monster to life. Gainesville is Florida's Basildon, and the hotel was sitting on a roundabout on their M25. Still, abroad's abroad, right?

Each day courtroom scenarios were set for us to reenact. The UK lawyers Tony Wyatt and Sam Magee were excellent. A trademark of the US attorneys was they seemed to want to use dramatic effect for its own sake, even if it harmed rather than helped. To them, more is always more.

'And then my client shot the victim three times,' said the attorney. 'Bang! Bang! Bang!'

'Er, yes,' I said, trying to assist, 'that is the prosecution's case. How does that help your client, may I ask?'

Reflecting for a moment, they sheepishly answered, 'I guess it doesn't.'

Sometimes both the advocacy and the tactical decision making may leave something to be desired. Now, I am not saying that the trial process is a game, as many a Judge has said to me. But it is between two sides and can be divided in two halves, and has a result, so what else is it? It is not rugby, and tackling another barrister around the legs might be frowned on, but it is not a million miles from chess, albeit checkmate of the Defendant may have more serious consequences than just laying down your king.

A glimpse at two decisions of American cases where Defendants did not give evidence will show you what I mean.

Dare I say his name? Harvey Weinstein. The world has heard little else than of the guilt of Harvey Weinstein in terms of the women he abused. He was reliant in his trial upon the old maxim that lightning can strike six times or even, possibly, eighty times and still be innocent.

But by the time he came to trial he was probably the first public enemy No. 1 since the robber John Dillinger though, unlike Dillinger, it was not his firearm that got him into trouble.

But if Weinstein was not prepared to give evidence, his reputation was so poor he would have no creditable prospect of being acquitted. Yet he chose not to.

Whilst he had limited success in knocking out the rape allegations, the remainder earned him twenty-three years in prison. Should he have given evidence? The answer, I suspect, is damned if you do and damned if you don't.

The same tactic of not giving evidence was used in the defence of Mike Tyson, former world heavyweight champion, in his trial for rape. Whilst he did not give evidence to rebut the allegation that he had taken someone to his hotel room and there raped her, he called witnesses to say he could not be guilty.

It is a poor tactic to not give evidence yourself but call others on your client's behalf. If he has something to say, let him say it himself, not get someone else to do it for him. It just highlights his having something to hide. And Mike Tyson being scared of giving evidence is not a good look for someone who is, arguably, the toughest guy ever to climb into the ring. That said, the decision to give evidence or not, whilst being something that can be advised on, is ultimately a matter for the Defendant.

There are some guiding, commonsense, forensic principles. Despite having the option, there are categories of Defendants that *should* be known for their integrity, e.g. a policeman, lawyer or priest (you can hear me clearing my throat after I mentioned each of them). These people are supposed to take oaths that mean something to them, and if they say they are innocent they should be able to look the Jury in the eye and swear it's true.

My conclusion of advocates and advocacy is as follows: if Carlsberg made British advocates, they would probably be the best in the world.

36.

In the dock

Time for a shout-out for the stars of the show: the accused. Sometimes, in fact, their shout-outs aren't of enormous assistance.

As we know, a word here or there can make all the difference: a client sitting in the dock, listening to a witness give evidence that implicated him, had the foresight to shout out, 'He should be in the dock with us.' Now, if he had had the foresight to shout, 'He should be in the dock *instead of us*', that I might have understood. But then, shouting in court, whether it be by Judge, witness or Defendant, usually achieves nothing.

During one of my closing speeches in Chelmsford Crown Court the Judge decided to rest his eyes.

'Oy, Judge, wake up – Nigel is speaking,' shouted the man in the dock.

As it happens, I didn't mind one bit that the Judge was resting his eyes. I wanted to say to the client, 'Don't worry, we aren't speaking to him anyway. So long as the Jury is awake ...' Mind you, in some cases a sleeping Jury isn't necessarily a bad thing either.

The expression 'I dined out on that story' has been applied to some raconteurs. If I dined out on each of my amusing stories, I would have saved quite a bit of money invested in Weight Watchers. I say invested, but the fridge magnet saying, 'That's the first stone lost,' has long since lost its attraction for the door.

The one tale I won't forget is holidaying – sorry, I mean, working – in Truro. Two men were being tried for drug importation in what I've described to you as a 'cut-throat'. One, having given evidence against his co-Defendant, made his way back to the dock and muttered something to his partner in crime.

A vigilant dock officer brought to the court clerk's attention that he had heard what was said and came forward to say he had heard the man returning to the dock saying 'There, that's the payback!' – i.e. revenge. It was important, as if he had said this it would indicate that, whilst not necessarily untrue, his account was based on pure spite and unlikely to be believed. The dock officer repeated on oath the words he had heard – 'There, that's the payback.'

I suggested to him that what might have been said was the genteel enquiry, 'Excuse me, is this the way back?'

For the 1,600th time in my life my suggestion was found unhelpful.

And finally on the topic of shout-outs, I was once explaining to a Jury what the case was about. I said that they may notice that in photograph no. 1 the Defendant was bald, whereas in photo no. 2 he was either wearing a wig or had a haircut given him by Ken Dodd's hairdresser. A growl from the dock arrived. 'That's fxxking funny,' said the Defendant on the left of the dock, hence answering the question as to who the man in the picture was.

All of the above simply enforces the wisdom of the expression, 'Least said, soonest mended.'

37.

The advocates

Courtroom dramas from *Rumpole of the Bailey* to *Kavanagh QC* have occupied our screens almost from the dawn of time, and reveal an endless appetite for legal dramas.

As spin-offs from crime trials, we have the police: both Inspectors Morse and Vera, with her green wellington boots, always get their man (and woman). The village of Midsomer has had so many murders that, apparently, by the end of series twenty-two, the last villager had been killed. Clearly, suicide was all that the script writers could offer Detective Inspector Barnaby. Having been apprehended, the suspects in these dramas get the choice of being tried by Judge Judy, Judge Deed or Judge Rinder.

This appetite of the public for crime and punishment has existed since before Dostoyevsky wrote, well ... *Crime and Punishment*. But within the courtroom, through fact and fiction, has stood the advocate pure and brave. Sometimes.

COMMUNITY CHEST

When I started, and for many years, the advocates for both prosecution and defence came from the ranks of the Bar. The reference to the barrister sitting in the advocate's row for the other team as 'my learned friend' is completely apposite. It contradicts the old John Cleese joke when he observed in a Monty Python mock trial that his learned friend was 'neither learned nor his friend'. In fact that is not correct. Your opponents might well be your friends. In my world, if friendship runs deep, so should loyalty.

Is everyone that is old, old-fashioned? The answer is probably yes, however much they protest.

I love communities, and the Bar is a great community.

It should operate – and usually does – on allegiance and trust. Do you remember the red and blue bags I referred to as identifying badges of the Bar? When I was a 'baby Barrister' I remember having to get a train to court and turning up at Victoria Station with my blue bag over my shoulder. I was running late and there was a very long queue at the ticket office. There, second place in the queue, stood a woman with her blue bag in hand. On being asked, she immediately agreed to buy me a ticket to wherever.

Another example of how the community thing worked was when one barrister was going through domestic hell. He had formed a relationship with someone new, although he was neither legally nor emotionally free to do so. That said, the only thing remaining of his marriage was its existence. It was a shell, and he was racked with guilt about it. He had not just begun to drink but was becoming a hopeless alcoholic (unlike a lot of other barristers, who were hopeful alcoholics). His work was affected. What was remarkable was that, within the constraints of our duties to our clients, we all did what we could to shoulder his burden and carry him, as if we were carrying him from the dark place he was in to a lighter place. We realised our professional relations with our clients were important, but our relationship with our friend was so much more.

That said, the case we were doing did have its funnier side. A woman was encouraged to come over to the house where her ex-husband still lived with their young son. He enticed her by a phone call on the pretext that the child had a headache.

When she arrived, she was unaware he had raised the floorboards and dug out an area to accommodate her soon-to-be-dead body. The police somehow intervened and he was arrested.

At his trial she gave evidence of his bad character. Apart from his apparent hobby of archaeology and tunnelling, she said he was an inveterate gambler. In defence of his client, our friend suggested he confined gambling to 'a few stocks and shares'.

She was mortified. 'Stocks and shares? Stocks and shares? He bet on horses, dogs, cats; two flies up the wall he'd have a punt.'

But not everyone was blessed with community spirit. I saw a different friend of mine who had struck the big four: mental fragility, divorce, loss of a parent and cancer, being treated with the sensitivity of a wrecking ball by his chambers. It would have been so easy to carry him. In any community of a hundred or so, a number will need propping up. It is how we treat them wherein we are judged.

THE VOICE

The most serious cases were conducted by the big beasts of the Bar – organised crime and high-profile murders, prosecuted and defended by the best-known Silks and Juniors. QCs who were Big Beasts with Big Booming Voices, who filled a room and spellbound juries. It was Marshall Hall KC in the 1920s or Jeremy Hutchinson (who defended Christine Keeler and the rights to publish *Lady Chatterley's Lover*) in the 1960s. But there have been some big beasts in my era too. Their big characters tended to be accompanied by big, sonorous voices.

Here is a thumb sketch of just some of them from my era of BBBs (Big Booming Barristers). These were my role models, who helped me learn my craft.

Brian Higgs QC just filled a courtroom. He was a towering figure, and had an amazing presence. As we were both known in Essex, we were often put in harness together, with him leading me. This was remarkably reassuring for both me, who could shelter behind his gown, and for the Essex public, who could shelter behind him. But from time to time, we were against each other. Truth be told, that was quite difficult, as I was in awe of him.

He prosecuted me (as we say) in a murder that had taken place on hospital grounds. I was instructed by a garrulous solicitor named Bernie, of whom I was very fond – he would bounce around the place, perhaps speaking too much, as he had the enthusiasm of a nine-month-old red setter.

Our client had a speck of blood on a shoe, and although it was forensically linked to the victim, I was optimistic the Defendant would be acquitted. One morning I saw Brian approaching me and I said to myself, 'I know what is coming. Brian is about to throw his hand in and offer no further evidence against my client.'

Instead, what he said was: 'If Bernie doesn't keep quiet, I'll have him arrested.'

Brian's advocacy was brilliant in that case – as ever – and one spot of blood sent my client for a spot of prison.

The second silky-smooth hero of mine was an old Silk named David Cocks QC, someone with whom one could happily spend a superabundance of time. At the end of the court day, we would lean over a gate in the field of my house in Thaxted. We looked like two characters devised by Harry Enfield. As with most people of his age, David was fearless and quick-witted.

The particular Judge he and I were before had clearly read and seen an image of a Judge at the turn of the century, but I don't mean the twenty-first or even the twentieth century, I mean the nineteenth century. Everything was made of cut glass, except the glass he drank from. His accent was cut-glass. His vocabulary was cut-glass and his clothing likewise. But with the cut-glass labelling, of course comes another label: 'Pompous twit'. The court was ideal for him. Wood-panelled and entirely old-fashioned, its acoustics made everything ring out as far as the neighbouring graveyard.

David Cocks QC took his place in court before the Judge had come onto the bench in front and, turning to me, said – not entirely quietly – 'This Judge is a complete tosser.'

Enter the Judge. 'Mr Cocks, you may have forgotten since your last visit the acoustics in this building are impeccable.'

David Cocks languorously turned to me, saying sufficiently loudly for the Judge to hear, 'See what I mean?'

Voices at the Bar are important. It leads to presence. But it can also lead to conviction. To the barristers above, their voices were blessings. To a client I had they were a curse. He truly had the deepest voice I had ever heard. He made Barry White sound like a castrato. All very well, except a witness to a murder identified him as having a completely distinctive, extraordinarily deep, voice. Such identification, albeit unusual, was in no way inadmissible.

It was true, and I could not see a way around it. The moment he opened his mouth in court, even to say 'Not guilty', he was a goner. I did not permit him to open his mouth in the presence of the Jury, and certainly not to give evidence. If the Jury heard him there would be but one verdict – which there was anyway.

Don't get confused between great voices and great presence on the one hand and posh voices with ludicrously strangulated vowels on the other. They are not the same. BBC newscasters no longer wear dinner jackets and black ties to read the news. They are not even all men, but neutral accents and interesting tones are another matter.

APPLES AND PEARS

A number of members of the Bar and, in my experience, fine members of the Bar – have Cockney accents. One friend, Colin Wells, does not give a moment's consideration to the perceived smarter accent that was the plight of some barristers. A West Ham supporter, his pronunciation was honed on the terraces of the North Bank, and he deservedly has had a very successful career. Even had he bothered, he could never disguise his most obvious qualities of thorough charm and decency.

One practitioner might have overstepped credulity, but I really enjoyed her appearing before me at the Old Bailey, when I sat as a Recorder (an old term for a part-time Judge – not the musical instrument). She was cross-examining a witness in a not-very-serious assault case, and was suggesting that the club bouncer was interested in a woman on the dancefloor.

'Did you get her digits?' she asked.

I looked to confirm that the press were not there. 'Did you *what*, Ms X?'

'Get her digits, My Lord.'

I was now feigning ignorance and playing to the absent gallery.

'Ask for her phone number,' she needlessly explained.

I went into pompous mode: 'Please, Ms X, this is not a bowling alley.'

CHARM

It must have become clear by now that strength of character and straightforward dealing get you a long way in life. The same goes at the Bar. When all else fails in argument, use charm. In fact, use charm anyway. Charm is courtesy and kindness's first cousin. It never harmed anyone in any walk of life. It cannot overcome ignorance, but it can help, playfully, to disguise it.

Also, leg-pulling is a virtue; indeed, in my case, it would have assisted in my final settled height.

Dorian Lovel Pank QC was a shortish, dandyish, beautifully coiffured advocate – I used to imagine that if I was well-behaved and morally upright, I would be resurrected as Dorian. He was charm personified. I rivalled him in shortness of height. At 5'7" I was well over a foot shorter than my client. Mr Johnson truly was seven foot. When I spoke to him, he would kneel in the dock at the Old Bailey whilst I stood by it, and hence we were the same height.

In their opening remarks to the Jury, the prosecutor customarily introduced each of the Defendants and who represented them. Dorian introduced me and the client to the Jury by saying, 'Mr Johnson, the tallest man in the dock, is represented by my learned friend Mr Lithman, who is ...' dramatic pause for him to say shortest counsel, and for me to pull myself up in stilettoes but out he came with, '... counsel at the end of the row.'

MUSCLE

The final category to mention of useful qualities in an advocate is muscle. There are some who could have been in the boxing ring – and others who actually were.

Tony (barrister and author Tony Kent) was different to your average barrister. Tony was an ex-boxer. He had sparred with some of the UK's finest. He was the thinking man's Tyson Fury – not, for Heaven's sake, that Tyson Fury *isn't* the thinking man's Tyson Fury and, in any event, don't tell him I suggested it ...

I first saw Tony in action in the ring of the court-room. This was in Florida (previously mentioned) while he was representing the English Bar and I was part of the judging panel. In the court re-enactments, I watched him dispose of his American opponents as if they were featherweights in his heavyweight division. Some time later, when involved in prosecuting a case, I said to myself, 'Blimey, I need protection here.' Whilst the court building may have security it is not always immediate enough.

I was cross-examining the Defendant, an enormous man. As we approached the end of the day, I said to him, 'I have one topic left, which I will deal with tomorrow.'

I proposed to ask him about his previous offending and jail terms. I reckoned when I asked him about it, there was a good chance he would thump me. However lithe I am – which is as lithe as an LG refrigerator in one of the small courts at Chelmsford – he would be on me before I could get out of the way. I asked Tony if he would join my case team for the day, and explained why.

He said, 'Don't worry, Nige. When he makes his move, just step sideways. I'll step in and deck him.'

Next day, Tony came and took his position behind me. I asked the question, 'It's right, isn't it, that in 1982 you went to prison for attempted murder?' Sharp step sideways.

No reaction.

The guy looked, saw what was going on and just smiled. He knew exactly what I had proposed doing, and knew the best way to deal with the point was just brush it aside. But then maybe having Tony sitting behind me and casting a shadow over the rear half of the court had something to do with it.

LEGENDS

Whilst Malory's *Morte d'Arthur* had Sir Lancelot and Sir Galahad as its heroes, the Bar had someone whose name I had better abbreviate by the initials J.O. A coincidence, as one of the best-known events he was involved in included the letters F.O.

He managed to turn naïveté and candour into an art form.

Once asked why he was late into court, he told the Judge he had been 'mugging up the law', as if another fifteen minutes would give him a compendium-type knowledge. In truth, we suspected that this was the first time he had mugged up anything. It wasn't the first time he'd needed help.

In the course of one trial, he decided that he would ask the Judge for a 'bit of advice'. Whatever else Judges do to counsel – possibly shout, even threaten to report them to their professional body – the one thing they won't do for counsel is give them a 'bit of advice'. But being taken aback by the frankness of J.O., the Judge tried to be helpful. 'Mr O., I am afraid I can't give counsel advice, but I see that in the rows of counsel are many illuminati of the profession. For instance, why not ask Sir Lionel Thompson? In the finest traditions of the Bar, I'm sure he will help.'

Back came the answer, 'I did ask Sir Lionel, M'Lord. He told me to fxxk off.'

OFF THE RECORD

Crown Court proceedings are a matter of record. Before recording machines came stenographers and before typewriters came quills and ink. During the transition period between humans and machines came the use of both. Humans would come and change the tape when it had run out. Fine work if you could get it.

There was a time during a trial at the Old Bailey that I was making a submission in law to the Judge. As is the custom, the Jury had retired to ensure they did not hear that which would prejudice them against the Defendant (they cannot unhear what they have heard). The Judge had been extraordinarily difficult, both with me and my client. Things looked bleak.

Me: My Lord, I would like to submit …
Judge: Mr Lithman, would you pause, please, for a few moments, whilst we bring in the person to change the tape?

I weighed up the situation.

Me: Certainly, but do I understand that at this moment nothing is being recorded in any way?

Judge: That is correct.

Me: What, no record – whatever?

Judge: None.

Me: Than may I take this opportunity of thanking your lordship for your great fairness and courtesy in overseeing this trial?

Judge (smiling): Would you like to repeat that in a few minutes, on the record?

Me (with bigger smile): Certainly not.

AN EVEN PLAYING FIELD

Nowadays, the tradition that advocates come only from the Bar has changed and often include those coming from the other side of the profession. Solicitors thus perform what are two roles: preparation of the case and, on occasion, engaging a solicitor advocate rather than counsel to represent the client in court. Two roles may mean two fees ('double bubble') – one for the preparation and one for the advocacy. The roles often overlap, either when done by the same person or with a clearer than glass ceiling between the two.

The Bar was slow to react or respond effectively when the courtroom monopoly they had always enjoyed was eroded – by and large, the Bar side of the profession appears unable to organise something in a something. The words escape me.

But clearly whilst the Bar was having breakfast and weren't paying full attention, a kookaburra swooped down and flew off with their bread and butter. By the time the Bar realised what was happening, they had lost their monopoly; it was too late. Large solicitor firms were able to deal with whole lists of cases in a court, and many of them employed ex-barristers to undertake the advocacy for them. From some barristers' viewpoint this could be an attractive proposition, particularly for those who preferred a wage as an employee rather than having to meet the expenses of the self-employed, but the remainder saw what had been their cake being eaten by someone else, whilst only crumbs were left.

Whatever led to blurring the distinction between the traditional roles of the barrister and solicitor in the courtroom, there is a part each can play in ensuring proper legal representation for those who find themselves in the dock. Especially for those who fall through the gap without legal aid or representation. I have found the presence of solicitor advocates in the court building an advantage (how things change!), and appreciate their willingness to go and speak informally to the Defendant. Some will turn into paying clients, many will not.

The real problem I see, however, is to ensure there are sufficient numbers of independent, highly trained and effective advocates for the future. And when the costs of training on both sides of the profession are so high, and the levels of remuneration so low that the advocates have to scrap for their livelihoods (they are expected to do more and more without payment and do so only due to their own professional integrity), there is a real concern that entry will become barred except to those who can afford it. All the important work over many years to open access to the legal profession, to attract the best and brightest candidates, promote diversity and ensure the highest quality of advocates will be lost.

This is a drum I have banged before, when leading the Criminal Bar in its fight with the government of the day. If you keep reading, you'll find the detail.

38.

Twelve good citizens

It has taken many pages, but at last we come to it: the probable answer to injustice and the antidote to potential unfairness.

If I have shown that barristers and solicitors, in order to do an exceptionally stressful job, may be indifferent to the question of the guilt of their clients and Judges might begin the trial process with a dose of scepticism, how come Defendants can still have a fair trial? Answer: the Jury. The Jury is also the body in each trial that makes the Judge's personal views redundant.

It is the independence of the Jury system that every lawyer and every Judge with even half a belief in justice would not change. During our plague of coronavirus, the Scottish courts flirted for a millisecond with the idea of doing away with the Jury system and replacing it with Judge-only trials. I suspect the suggestions were based on speed, case backlog and social distancing. The responses were based on democracy, custom and the rule of law. The idea was dropped quicker than it had been picked up.

It is for the Jury to play the most important part in a criminal trial and to grapple with the decision-making process, whilst being fairly and properly directed. Some of what they are told by the Judge will include:

a They must follow the oaths they take at the beginning of the trial.
b They must not reach verdicts based on sympathy for one side or the other (hence they too should shelve any moral turpitude the case may visit on them).
c They should not speculate about anything they have not heard during the trial – and especially not undertake any research on the internet or via the news media.
d They should not leave their common sense outside the courtroom.

There are many reasons to believe that the process is a good one. Twelve citizens, all independent of each other, come together to hear the evidence. Within the Jury are people very familiar with the two best friends 'nitty 'and 'gritty', and are able to drill down to the essence of the case. They bring their own common sense and experience to their task. They *will* be true to their oaths, the oath being that they swear or affirm to try the case according to the evidence. Even if all of their instinct tells them he is guilty, if the evidence ain't there, it ain't there. Forgive my using the word 'ain't', but I noticed Ed Milliband used that expression at the same time as eating a bacon sandwich. It must be OK for me to do the same (use the word 'ain't', that is). Whilst being true to their oaths, they will keep at least two eyes on what is just and come up with the 'right' result.

THE BOBBLE HAT

I have described how more than sometimes there was war between cops and robbers. In the trials that ensued it was as if the Jury were set up to intercede between them. One Defendant became involved in a particularly personal, long-running feud with a policeman. It became a show of strength. He wanted to send a message and chose a message in a bottle. The bottle was a Molotov cocktail, and the message he hoped to send would reach the house occupants, husband, wife and children asleep upstairs. Sometime later, having started a fire that was, fortunately, contained, he was arrested.

There was evidence in the case, but for me one of the pieces did not hang straight. In front of the house was a dustbin. It stood there for all the world and the police to see. When the police first attended, they found nothing of note in the front of the house. They returned two days later and then found a bobble hat in the bin, and this was said to contain a scientific link to the arsonist.

As it was a policeman's house you would expect the preliminary search to have revealed it. How was it missed? In my closing address I listed all of the abundant reasons as to why this evidence did not ring true, and like the flower bed in the front garden, smelt of a plant, and it was not a hydrangea. But the Jury convicted. Why? Because that is their right. You cannot second-guess a Jury; there will be many cases such as this where, despite holes or doubts in the evidence, looked at overall, they have no doubt as to guilt.

Equally, there are many cases where they will exercise their judgement and common sense in the opposite direction and, even in the teeth of a compelling piece of evidence, they will express a total unwillingness to convict on it.

39.

The pubic hair and the rapist

'You can lead a Jury to water – but you can't make them convict.'

Following an allegation of rape, a complainant was taken to the police station to make her allegation, to take off her clothes and subject herself to providing swabs whilst her clothes were 'forensicated' (what a vile word), looking for clues of association, hair, fibres, etc.

She was asked to surrender her clothes and stood on a very large brown evidence bag in order to do so.

As she took off her clothing, at some stage, seen by the attendant officers, like a petal of blossom in spring, a single pubic hair fluttered down onto the brown bag. I do not know how many pubic hairs we have, and frankly I cannot say I have ever counted them, or whether women have the same number as men, but the one that fluttered down was a single one and a male one, and it bore the DNA of the Defendant. The prosecution used the help of the FBI to assist its science.

The way DNA works is to invest a proportion of likelihood, e.g. 'If the hair bears the DNA of the

Defendant, what are the chances it came from someone else?' A common answer is one in a billion. But
chances can increase.

The Defendant had an explanation. He knew the
Complainant, but not well, and at one stage claimed
that the hair must have dislodged inexplicably and
attached itself to the Complainant when they had
both visited the same site, albeit not together.

Or alternatively, a hair had become dislodged at
the site, wafted its way across the dunes of Essex,
hit a wall at the police station, made its way up the
wall and entered the window of the forensicating
room at exactly the same time as the Complainant
was getting undressed and, with the grace of a flying
carpet, landed on the brown paper bag.

There was, of course, another explanation: that
the rapist left it on the woman as he raped her.

My close friend John Dodd – now a QC and Judge
– whom I was leading in the case, came up with the
idea that if you took the Jury to view the scene where
the Defendant had his picnic and dislodged his pubic
hair, the Jury would dismiss the flight of fantasy as
ridiculous. My view was that they could do this without trekking down to a windy dune in Essex. Why
would a Jury accept a fanciful account that flew in
the face of scientific certainty or indeed that a single
pubic hair would fly in the face of the police station?
The answer is almost certainly, they did not. But to
convict a man of rape on the strength of one pubic

hair clearly offended against certainty. Sometimes, things are what they are.

The area of sexual offending is well known to be both a legal and factual minefield. I have had to learn to slalom through the areas of evidence to try and accomplish whatever my brief asks, or in order to hold the ring as the Judge. I have experienced these cases in all of their guises at every stage of my career. This includes battered wives syndrome, which led a wife to say to her husband, 'I can take no more.' Acquitted of murder after she'd stabbed him, in fact she'd stabbed him in the kitchen, along the hallway and for good measure in the living room. Notwithstanding that in strict legal terms neither self-defence nor provocation would have applied, that did not stop the Jury in my view rightly acquitting her. Self-defence does not have to be stationary.

Don't get me wrong, I am not unconditionally in love with the Jury system. The praise above for it does not mean they are necessarily consistent or predictable. That is part of the attraction. For instance, when I was young and could pass as better-looking, I prosecuted a trial in Canterbury Crown Court. Having heard my speech for the Crown and my opponent's for the defence, as the Jury withdrew to their retirement room, one who filed past me with the others gave me a thumbs up. I had no doubt therefore that they would convict. Sure enough, fifteen minutes later the Jury filed back and the foreman announced, 'Not guilty'!

As a Judge it became most apparent how low the conviction rate for sexual crime was. Sitting up high, surveying the arena from the Judge's vantage point, very often leads to my incredulity. The safeguards built into the system, in theory, permit a Jury to hear a Complainant's evidence in its most natural light. The Complainant can give her testimony in a pre-recorded police interview. This can be played to the Jury through TV monitors, whilst the Complainant sits in another room. She will then be cross-examined by the Defendant's counsel, either via the link or in the courtroom, often behind screens.

These are special measures, designed to attain the best evidence given in the most relaxed way. These days a Defendant can't wade through evidence deemed to show her in her worst light (how she dressed; how she has behaved in the past), unless strictly relevant. Additionally, fairness is built into the summing up by the Judge: no assumptions of stereotype.

But notwithstanding this, again and again, where the case depends upon the Jury being able to say which of the two accounts given is true, if it is one person's word against another, they will consistently acquit.

As I have indicated, the Jury are not always predictable. To them also applies the epithet, 'There's nowt as queer as folk.'

40.

Lock, stock and two smoking barrels

Thaxted, where I lived, is situated next to Great Dunmow, a market town, with its beautiful old wine shop with ebony timbers and a supermarket run by the Co-op.

Into the car park of that supermarket one day drove the cash collection security van, where it was met by a reception party. The party between them had a sawn-off shotgun, which, it was alleged – and ultimately proved – was discharged by my client into the security car driver's leg, blowing it off.

The trial ran for about a month, and in that time, of course, the Jury – as is the anachronism of the system – said nothing, and we the lawyers and the Judge said everything. Whatever I said was not going to get my client acquitted, and his co-accused, represented by Anthony Berry QC with Michael Logsden, was all but certainly going to suffer the same fate. So it was: they were both convicted, receiving substantial prison sentences. Our client was convicted 11–1, which seemed like a pretty good result. We had persuaded someone. Or had we?

The conferences we had with our client were not the happiest of events, as it seemed pretty apparent that the bathing facilities of the prison did not allow him to properly wash his long hair, which rivalled our wigs for lustre.

My Junior, Jim, and I packed our belongings and bade our client farewell. The arrangement barristers have with their clients is quite strict – you take all the fee and they take all the prison.

But on our way out we were called back to the court. The Prosecutor, Chris Moss QC, later to become an Old Bailey Judge, had heard that a person had been to the general office at the court to see if she could get some appeal forms to enter for the Defendant. The said person was recognised as someone who had sat on the Jury. It was, to say the least, slightly bizarre for a juror to seek to help the person to appeal when they had just convicted him. Inquiries were made of the prison, and it emerged that the same juror had, in the middle of the trial, obtained forged passes to visit him in prison.

The reason behind her infatuation bemused me. After all, why would a young woman juror fall in love with someone whose talents seemed to extend as far as shooting a man's leg off but not quite as far as shampooing his hair? Anyway, love is strange.

I used the episode to launch an appeal on behalf of the Defendant. One of the tests for an appeal was whether there was a material irregularity in the trial process. I would have thought that there could be no greater irregularity than one of the jurors visiting the Defendant in prison. My argument ran that one could have no proper way of knowing what influence her bias had on the other jurors. Like Mummy, the Court of Appeal knew better. She had no influence on the rest of them whatever, they announced, hence the verdict was a proper one of 11–1. And we all knew who the one was, did we not?

On the Bench, all of the Lords of Appeal were Scottish, and their names all began with 'Mc'. It was like the cast of *Braveheart*, and they treated me in the same way as they would have William Wallace, who wiggled his bottom at his enemy. That night we agreed to meet up with our co-defending counsel, Tony, for an end-of-case dinner. Tony was staying in a smallish hotel, which I had eaten in before. He is one of the characters who would deserve mention in any tale such as this. He was very funny, faux-posh and had a distinctive cough in the form of throat clearance that preceded him into any room. As I gauged that he would be used to fine-dining standards, which this hotel could not provide, we agreed to meet at 8 p.m., but my last words were 'Don't expect haute cuisine; it's the sort of place where you can choose between either gammon on its own or gammon with pineapple on top.'

We met. We sat down. A fourteen-year-old, part-time schoolgirl waitress arrived. 'Got any lobster?' Tony bellowed.

PART 8

Checks and balances

41.

Changing the odds

If the presence of juries in the system creates a balance of justice that Judges could not, the same effect has been achieved by various Acts of Parliament throughout the ages.

The year 1984 brought a seminal moment, as regulation of arrests, police custody and interviews were made subject to review by the courts. In that year, as previously mentioned, the Police and Criminal Evidence (PACE) Act instituted a legislative framework for powers of the police to combat crime, as well as codes of practice to establish a balance between those powers and the rights and freedoms of the public.

The 2003 Criminal Justice Act sought to introduce previous 'no go' areas of evidence into trial proceedings. Even those that had sat at the back of every lecture they ever attended – even they could not be unaware of the significance of 2003. It would be like saying that, whilst P.G. Wodehouse's character Jeeves might not have known who the participants were, even he would have known that sometime around 1939 there had been a world war.

The Criminal Justice Act 2003 might be seen as a 'balancing up' between the admissibility of evidence hitherto largely kept away from the public and how a Judge should oversee its introduction.

One interpretation of what had happened was a realisation that the law had become imbalanced in favour of the Defendant by the Jury being deprived of hearing evidence that common sense suggested ought to be admitted.

Hitherto a trial resembled an iceberg – not the lettuce, but the one that had Leonardo Di Caprio in the sea, whilst Kate Winslet floated on a door.

It was the norm that before 2003 a case was heard absent of clearly relevant material, which might be deemed prejudicial against the Defendant. Further, the defence were ordinarily deprived of 'unused material' touching upon the case, for instance who else had been investigated, and with what results.

The year 2003 helped to balance things up.

Prior to that, a Jury might well have concluded the trial without knowing that the Defendant was a repeat serial offender and acquit a Defendant in ignorance of what the Judge and counsel would know of his history. Should they not, in certain circumstances and with ample safeguards against jumping to conclusions, be entitled to know this?

It used to be that if a Defendant attacked the character of a witness, he would lose the shield that protected him against the Jury hearing of his record, but save that it would rarely happen. Allowing evidence of somebody's previous convictions, particularly when the information could lead to overwhelming prejudice and the conclusion 'he has done it before, hence it follows that he has done it again' was generally not permitted. You couldn't give a dog a bad name and then hang him by it. Meanwhile, if the Defendant was a man of good character, the Jury would be told that repeatedly.

Was that fair?

The reality was that fairness was deemed only to apply to the defence. Henceforth, it was to be a two-way street – for defence and prosecution. This applied not just to the bad character of the Defendant, but also to witnesses and third parties.

At the same time as bad character creeping into trials, hearsay evidence was also to be admitted, subject to rules. Historically, if you were to ask counsel for a definition of 'hearsay', they would be likely to say a reality TV band. Criminal textbooks have spent chapters on hearsay. This is not a legal textbook, but I suppose the simplest example is if a witness in a murder trial says that he heard a man say he saw the accused stab the victim to death. If this is to be relied on for the truth of that which the man said, that is hearsay. If you doubt this, feel free to consult Dr Google. I previously said he has a degree in every medical speciality; it turns out he also has an MA and LLM in Law from both the Universities of Oxbridge and London.

If someone had committed an offence in perfect secrecy, then even if there were hearsay references to the crime implicating the Defendant, it would often be kept from the Jury.

The year 2003 set out the evidential circumstances in which these anachronisms were corrected, and the Jury could hear of these features, albeit the Judge must now direct them that they should not convict wholly or largely because of them.

The beauty of the changes, if they could possibly be called beautiful, was that it remained with my friends the Jury as to how they reacted to hearing this material. I doubt one can ever go too far, but I have seen some pretty smart verdicts from them.

I twice represented alleged double-killers. That's right, different victims, different trials, different times. How unlucky is that? Some of us aren't even arrested once for murder, never mind twice. In each of the first pair of cases I led an exceptionally tall and exceptionally funny barrister called Ben Hargreaves. Ben is Jenny Eclair's brother. I have always maintained that he is even funnier than his stand-up comedian sister (no disrespect to Jenny and, to be fair, I haven't heard her in the cells at the Old Bailey doing one of her routines). Ben himself also does stand-up, but wears a wig and gown as he does it. He always kept me in hysterics. With his art of charm and conversation he attacked with the gusto of someone on amphetamines. At the end of trial no. 1

the Defendant was acquitted. Notwithstanding that lightning never strikes twice, guess what? It did.

Who would have believed it, when fate delivered a second, crushing blow that put him in the Old Bailey dock, again charged with murder? Ben, still just as tall, and I had a rerun. The result was the same. Not guilty. Fortune smiled on the brave.

Meanwhile, a Judge sat watching this open-mouthed, as a man was acquitted twice for the same offence without a Jury knowing he had previously also been tried for murder. They weren't told, as previously he had been acquitted, and so was presumed as innocent as the day is long – well, certainly a day like 22 December in the UK or in mid-winter in the Antarctic.

What happened to this man? There are of course groups of people who find conventional justice inadequate. Someone shot him.

My second alleged double murderer was different, in that he was convicted the first time and spent twelve years in prison for killing a woman. When I met him, he was to be tried for killing another woman. The Crown claimed – and the Judge agreed – that the law permitted them to rely on his earlier conviction as evidence against him on the second, as the hallmarks for each bore a striking similarity. For instance, each woman was about fifteen years older than him, albeit, given the gap in time it meant that whilst one victim was in her thirties the other was in her fifties.

Apart from being proportionally older than himself, in the second trial there was another piece of striking evidence. The Defendant claimed he had not been to the victim's house for a month. In the house was found an undated newspaper. However, within the newspaper was an inserted advertisement that was dated and had been printed during the week of her murder. Upon that flyer was found the Defendant's fingerprints. Surely, collapse of defence? No. Despite hearing that he had killed a woman previously in very similar circumstances, the Jury did not convict him a second time. I am sure this Jury were worried about whether they would have been driven to convict purely by the previous conviction. Good for them.

42.

Technicalities

Why is 'twelve men and women good and true' the best system?

   a They tend to get it right.
   b By and large, almost all trials are essentially straightforward.

However complicated the subject matter might be, you can generally get to the heart of it in a trice.

GUINNESS IS GOOD FOR YOU – BUT NOT FOR ALL OF THEIR DIRECTORS

In the 1980s, the directors of Guinness were charged with fraud. The actual allegation was fraud relating to involvement in a conspiracy to drive up the price of Guinness shares during the drinks company's £2.6 billion attempt to take over Distillers in 1986.

   On the face of it – complicated? No. As one of my friends said, 'All that meant is that they had their hands in the till ...' and, sure enough, the Jury convicted them of what was essentially a very straightforward crime.

Even where lawyers can barely understand the technicalities of a case, a Jury may have no difficulty in discharging their duty.

NO SMOKE WITHOUT MURDER

I appeared with my good friend Gelaga King in a murder trial at Chelmsford Crown Court. Now, there's a surprise.

A woman had been killed and, hopelessly, in order to disguise the crime, was set fire to and left in a ditch. The Defendant was arrested in his car, where he had been asleep. The car reeked of smoke, but the police were well aware that a Jury might not convict if they merely had the police officer's word for the fact that the car stank. They turned for guidance to the FBI, who told the Essex police that they had previously done scientific work involving the chemical compounds deposited by soot on the Defendant and in his car. Apparently, a laboratory investigation could assess the extent suspended particles of soot could absorb the gas formaldehyde. The results obtained in experimental conditions showed that soot particles could bind 2.3 to 50.2 per cent of formaldehyde (I think we all know that).

In turn, formaldehyde is a colourless, strong-smelling gas used in making very many materials, including household products. It is used in pressed-wood products, such as particle board, plywood and fibreboard; glues and adhesives; permanent press fabrics; paper product coatings; and certain insulation materials. Hence, a product may have properties that indicate soot has settled on it.

Now, those are just words.

As I was about to embark in defence of this trial, I knew some of these words, but not what they meant.

Trials kicked off at 10.30 a.m. At 10.28, I was in the loo paying my usual, ninth, pre-trial nervous visit. 'What is this case about?' I whispered to myself. There were three cubicles in the men's and I was in trap two.

I suddenly heard, sotto voce, a familiar voice: 'What is this case about?'

After some loud flushing and other formalities, we met by the sinks. From trap one had come the prosecuting barrister. We both laughed and recognised that the experts were going to have to earn their money in this case.

That said, the Jury put all the evidence together and came up with a result neither of us could criticise. What was their verdict? I do remember but shall not say because the questions – whether they were happy with the clarity of the science or unhappy with its novelty or said a smoky car said it all – were all open to the Jury to conclude, and which they chose was entirely up to them.

So, a Jury can spot a soot deposit a mile off: they can also spot rubbish when it is being spoken to them.

FAIRY TALES

It is settled law that a Judge has to remind a Jury of the defence in a case, however fanciful it may seem objectively.

This is the verbatim reply of Jim Ageros QC when I asked him to recall one of the more ridiculous trials we did together:

'The S. brothers. I can't remember their first names but I'm ninety-nine per cent sure this was their surname. These were two brothers who were arrested by police officers in a caravan, counting out a very large sum of money on the table. The police were able to link the money with the armed robbery of a bank that had occurred a short time earlier in the near vicinity.

'The S. brothers' account was that they had been driving back to the caravan, minding their own business, when they were accosted by two men who seemed somewhat agitated and asked them to mind a large holdall. On inspection it turned out to be full of money. Being obliging types, they agreed.

'When asked to give a description of the two men, they were unable to, but given a few minutes described two men who referred to each other by the nicknames "Jumbo" and "Geordie".

'The significance of this was that the only description the terrified bank staff could give of the two robbers, who were both wearing masks, was that one was a large man and the other spoke with a north-eastern accent. That must be why they had the nicknames "Jumbo" and "Geordie", our clients surmised.

'This was the account the brothers gave to the Jury, an unbelieving bunch who rejected it.'

FAITH

My very last case at the Bar, however, confirmed that my faith in the Jury system may well be justified.

I have never made a secret of the fact that I am Jewish. Although Jews rarely get into trouble for violence, it is right that some of my co-religionists have not been strangers to fraud. Indeed, I know it to be true that a kindergarten class were once visited by a community relations police officer to talk about the fight against crime.

'So, what is crime?' asked the policeman.

After a long silence, a five-year-old put up his hand and said, 'Please, sir, is that what we call "insider trading"?'

Anyway, my last case before taking up my role as a Judge was to represent a charming man alleged to have been a knowing party to a bank fraud. Although he was an accountant to a number of the players, he had no part in the lavish lifestyle of his co-Defendants. The Jury, sensing his inner decency, had no hesitation in acquitting him. He was Jewish, as were his lead counsel (me), his junior counsel, Tim Kendal, and his solicitor, David Sonn. You would think that prejudice and stereotyping would make him an odds-on likely loser. Wrong. He was the only Jew in the dock and the only Defendant to be acquitted.

My faith in the Jury system is based on my experiences in the UK. Whether it would be replicated elsewhere I am not sure. I referred earlier in the book to my view of the superiority of our criminal justice system over America. I saw this highlighted when I was watching a rerun of *12 Angry Men* during our coronavirus period indoors. Henry Fonda talks round eleven jurors determined to find guilty a young man seen to have stabbed someone. He gets all eleven to change their minds. The evidence was clear – the recovered knife was unusual, with an ornate handle, and was recognised by an eyewitness. Indeed, a woman saw him stab the victim. With no evidential foundation whatever, our learned friend Henry (who it should be remembered had also previously played Abraham Lincoln in the movies, so himself must be no stranger to the law), persuaded the other eleven that the knife was so common, he himself had bought one and smuggled it into the Jury room, and the woman who had been asked no questions about it could not see unaided by glasses.

After nine hours and Lee J. Cobb changing his vote because he had problems with his own son, all twelve returned a verdict of not guilty. Damn, I've just missed giving a spoiler alert again.

I can assure you that in forty minutes that young man would have been convicted in England. This bunch speculated and invented evidence. The real reason he wasn't convicted in America was because of two words: 'electric' and 'chair'. And it was a movie. Undoubtedly, the abolition of capital punishment has freed up juries to do their duty as Judges of fact.

The final check and balance against an errant barrister or a rogue Judge is the Court of Appeal (unless of course they too are made up of formerly errant barristers and rogue Judges).

43.

A certain appeal

The Court of Appeal is the Big Brother (and sister) of the Crown Court. We, the Judges, know that if we mess things up that is where the case will be sent. How does a Judge get it wrong?

First, by making errors of law in decisions he gives during the course of the trial. For example if a Judge says it is right that the Jury can be told a Defendant has a previous conviction for unlawful possession of a knife, that would not be relevant for a Jury to hear during a charge of unarmed theft and would simply prejudice them against him. The Court of Appeal may well say that the Judge was in error by allowing that previous conviction to be introduced, and that the Defendant was convicted because of the prejudice that attached to him. We will quash the conviction and send him back to court to be retried or home to annoy and terrify his loved ones.

The test in appeals against conviction is, 'Is the conviction safe?'

However, don't expect the hearing to be loaded in favour of the appellant. After all, the Court of Appeal is made up of Judges. They too have grown up through the system. But, in their case, they will be acutely aware of other realities.

    a If every appeal is allowed, every case will be tried twice.

    b Reversal of decisions from the lower court may carry an inference of criticism of that court.

    c Does not the status quo always have an advantage? Just as it is easier for a barrister to knock something down than build it up, it is easier to leave things as they are than to change them.

The other large area where the Court of Appeal can interfere in a case is on sentence. Both teams can appeal. The defence can claim the sentence is 'manifestly excessive' and the prosecution can claim it is 'unduly lenient'. It may sound illogical, but it is not entirely unheard of that both parties can appeal, one saying the sentence is far too long, the other saying it is far too short.

As you would expect, there is a filter system. The grounds for appeal are set out in writing. Whilst the Court of Appeal usually sits with three Judges, before the case arrives in court it will be considered by a single Judge; if he decides there are arguable grounds and it is not just nonsense or a lawyer chancing his arm, he will let it go forward to be argued before the three of them.

Who does the arguing? Either the barrister or solicitor who conducted the trial, or one chosen for the purpose. Traditionally, Court of Appeal Judges were safely put in the ogre/tyrant/scary category, but as with all of them, as time passed, the more benign they either became or appeared to become.

Of course it is also an age thing. When I was at school in the early years, sixth-formers appeared to be aged somewhere between thirty-five and forty. That said, if you were quite thick and paying fees, they might well have been. In reality, they were probably eighteen.

I was in Southwark Crown Court some years ago, sitting alongside a QC called Tim Barnes. I asked him, 'Tim, why is it that, though I am nearly sixty, if I appear in the Court of Appeal tomorrow I will feel nervous butterflies in my stomach?'

His answer was spot on.

'For the same reason that I am sixty-four, Nigel, and going in front of the Supreme Court. It terrifies me. It is the one occasion we can be found out.' In other words, there is nothing to hide behind in the senior appeal courts. No Jury, just you and 'them'. If you are not on top of the case (and on top was not my usual position with case preparation), you will quickly be shamed, even though that is not their aim.

That said, I did used to wonder whether they had had raw meat for breakfast. But once the argument had started and it began to develop, of course, things relaxed.

Court 7 was usually the court to avoid. That is 'The Lord Chief Justice's Court', and one or two of the occupants of that seat or the seats alongside were truly ferocious.

'Mr Lithman,' barked Lord Justice Fred Lawton, 'how are English businessmen to hold up their heads in the international marketplace, when people like your client behave like this?'

I had not said a word. But that was that.

As the days arrived when I was old enough to be a Lord Justice of Appeal's father, my feelings of intimidation and 'imposter syndrome', along with my hair, receded further.

PART 9

Coping mechanisms

44.

Wellbeing and mindfulness

We have looked at the broad array of Defendants and the tales of terror in which we deal. The reason we have looked, albeit at just a small sample, is to appreciate why it might be that Judges and lawyers may have become inured to the sort of behaviour that sometimes bring the Defendants to court. If it just leads to nightmares that is one thing, but what about where the effects are greater?

The Criminal Courts, at a certain level, are just riddled with tales of awful horror, with each case exceeding its predecessor in its power to shock. I believe this contributes to a Judge's preliminary view of the people who come before him/her. But there is an equally important question: After all of this horror, how do barristers, solicitors and Judges cope?

Working amongst the ravages of mankind – if that is not too highfalutin' a way of expressing it – has promoted the importance of mindfulness and well-being in the criminal legal profession. The notion that the police, attending scenes of terrorism, murder and carnage, might need to have their own sensitivities cared for by counselling, has spread into the legal profession. Along with frontline police, criminal advocates and Judges are experiencing a diet of traumatic events daily. The idea took root that we could just shrug off our experiences.

During my career, I knew four people in the criminal justice system who, tragically, took their own lives. They were very different from one another, but all a joy to know, and the memory of them will live on long after we have forgotten all of the selfish egotists.

G.P. was the first truly fearless advocate I met. He was a big man and, unlike the observation of Michael Caine, appeared to be in shape. He had a really lovely, polished voice. I met him in Woolwich (in the Crown Court, not on the ferry). He became embroiled in an accusation that he had addressed a clerk inappropriately. I have no knowledge of the rights or wrongs of it, or if it contributed to an imbalance of mind that led to him later killing himself, but I do wish I might have been involved in his life to the extent that perhaps I could have done something to prevent what happened.

When the question is sometimes asked of us, 'Who would you have represent you if you got into trouble?', I have no hesitation in saying G.P. He was a great advocate. It never crossed my mind that he was anything other than totally believing in the case he was presenting. He was ego-free and decent and juries saw this in him. He would be my man.

L.B. was a gentle giant. He actually looked like Bluto, Popeye's adversary, but more kindly. He invited me to lead him on a number of occasions. We had a little in common, including that we both wore suits that never quite fitted. But he knew more law on more topics than I knew existed. He spoke warmly of his mother, but his father, a policeman, had died whilst he was young.

The other thing we had in common was an affinity for American history and politics, although, again, he outwitted me in knowledge of the subject a hundred-fold. After each case we did, I would receive a book on an American theme, such as the Kennedy brothers or Nixon. I learned one day he too had taken his own life.

We had appeared together in a case in Cambridge where a Defendant had murdered a stepbrother and decapitated him. The folly of the crime matched its awfulness.

How could we exclude that appearing in such cases had taken their toll on L.B.'s psyche?

It is a strange trait that people so able to advise upon the positions of others do not seem able to apply the same analysis to themselves.

That may, in part, be due to the fact that what we do is unreal. It exists on paper, as an academic or advocacy exercise. The tale of the specialist who can deal with his job so adeptly may be wholly incapable of marshalling the same skills and applying them to his own life. The creator of the surgeon Sir Lancelot Spratt in *Doctor in the House* (Richard Gordon) lived by the surgeons' motto 'when in doubt cut it out'. When the author contracted cancer, he refused surgery.

The third was a young and smiley Junior clerk in my chambers. I can only imagine that he fell into the blight that is the vulnerability of the young in our society. The fourth person I felt I knew well, though in reality I knew little. He too took his own life. He was a security officer at Luton Crown Court. He sat in the booth in the Judges' garage and greeted my late arrival every day with a chat and a smile. This was for the eighteen months I was there. We spend our lives at the Bar making judgements based on little: based on that little, I knew he was a really nice man and universally well-liked, and I am pleased to mention him here.

Life does not get too difficult sometimes just for the advocates to handle; unsurprisingly it can affect the Defendants as well, as they face up to the reality of what they have done. I have rarely been frightened during the job, but there were two or three occasions when I was threatened, and once the more so when the situation itself became hysterical, but not in a funny way.

Legally, the case was intricate. A woman and her partner were alleged to have abused her son, who was under their control. Three awful incidents of abuse amounted to torture. Tying the child to a tree far away from the house and leaving him there shivering and terrified until morning. Making him run on the spot and exercise until he was sweating, and then plunging him into a cold bath. He died of hypothermia. Straightforward torture.

The mother blamed the stepfather to the police. I, with my usual Junior, Jim, represented the stepfather, who predictably blamed the mother. The truth, I guess, was somewhere between the two of them. But the prosecution were only out to get the male. They accepted a mere plea to child neglect from the mother, but they did this deal only after her interview with the police was heard by the Jury. In that interview she blamed her partner. In law what one Defendant says about another is not evidence against that other, only against themselves. Wholly artificial, of course. If you blame someone often enough, it can stick. Remember 'That killer, Keith?' This stepfather's conviction for murder seemed inevitable.

But as the Crown's case finished, counsel for the Crown told me she would accept a plea of guilty to manslaughter from him and drop the murder. The difference between that plea (say, nine years, serve four and a half) and murder (say, twenty-three years and serve twenty-three years) was enormous. Do the math.

The duty of Jim and I was to try and make the stepfather see the wisdom of accepting the plea. He would not. He insisted he had done nothing at all wrong. Everything rationally showed otherwise. I could not let it lie there. It was too important. But the more I argued with him, the more hysterical he became. He paced around the room, smashing his fist against each of the four walls in turn. He shouted and cried. He turned the room into a living hell for all of us, but what he was going through was a scream to escape his situation.

He calmed down, but his views did not. I could not persuade him to see sense. Inevitably, he was convicted and received the long jail term. The noise and picture of that room stay with me … along with the porcelain child and all the dismembered bodies.

There is a need for wellbeing to be properly acknowledged and addressed in a kindly way by the legal profession. The profession has all of the -pathies in play: sociopathy on the one hand with sympathy and empathy on the other. Their relationship is the topic for a book of another discipline, but nothing is better placed than a kind and caring manner.

Wellbeing and mindfulness were beginning to occupy a place in our profession, and I was proud to promote it during my period as Chairman of the Criminal Bar. The notion that we should just battle our way through emotional problems was becoming less fashionable, although one can still hear the sneer sometimes in its discussion.

I have mentioned the excellent barrister Valerie Charbit (who falls squarely into the 'If you want something done well, ask a busy person' bracket). She, notwithstanding her busy sophisticated practice, has done more to promote the understanding of a need for wellbeing at the Bar and on the Bench than anyone I know.

It seems to me the difficulty remains twofold: recognition and dealing with it. Predictably, every aspect and degree of mental disorder feature in the criminal law, both in the perpetrators of crime as well as those that oversee its administration.

An example of the intricacies of cases where mental health are at their core arose when Valerie Charbit and I represented an eighteen-year-old suffering from Asperger's syndrome. He had been convicted of murdering his twelve-year-old cousin. The pathologist was unhappy about the outcome. The point that he wanted dealt with was a subtle one. The Jury had not been presented with the positive assertion that the victim had been choked by a ligature, which is what he believed had happened. This would have opened up the possibility that what had taken place was an accident occasioned during horseplay and be more consistent with manslaughter than murder.

The family instructed Val and me to take on the appeal. It was a worthy appeal and one wanted to say that the best point was that unusually in my gut I believed the verdict to be wrong. The cause of death was not the only aspect of the case that warranted revisiting. There was also a good alternative suspect and a real doubt as to whether the Defendant had committed the crime. Using barrister shorthand: this felt like it was a manslaughter case and not a murder case. It didn't feel right.

And these were just two of the points. The third was the nature and effects of the syndrome from which he suffered. The Jury had not been told what effect Asperger's had had on this Defendant. They had been left entirely uninformed as to how they should deal with this topic. The young man's father said his son's condition meant he was loath to leave his side and, as he did not on the night in question, he could not have killed his cousin. In other words, he was afforded an alibi for most, if not all of the evening.

It was, to say the very least, disappointing that the Court of Appeal would not accept any of these appeal points. As I've said, their ultimate test is, 'Is this conviction safe?' Not for the first time, Counsel for the Defence disagreed with their conclusion, and so this young man would spend many of his best years in jail.

45.

Hypochondria

I went through my own wellbeing crisis fifteen and more years ago. I became a complete hypochondriac. Not just in the Woody Allen, usual Jewish way; I simply refused to be assured that I was well. Now, I know that even hypochondriacs get ill, but mine was clearly a form of depression brought on by stress.

Doctors run in some families. In mine they practically gallop. I had access to countless doctors, relatives, friends, friends of relatives and children with chemistry GCSEs. I exhausted them all and myself. I would not have got through this without Debbie my wife, and Jim.

Jim and I were doing a case in Liverpool together, a fraud. It felt so far away from home. It was so far away from home. But as a matter of regularity, I would leave court to see any Liverpool GP or London specialists I had not yet seen – a quickly diminishing number. I needed constant reassurance, which, of course, I never accepted.

My brother-in-law recommended to me a specialist GP called Milton Maltz in Harley Street. Milton, a Brazilian with an amazing sense of humour, had the most disarming manner and, boy, did he need it with me. I once went through a *Carry On* film sketch while sitting in his waiting room.

I overheard him saying, 'I don't want the operation to go ahead today' – because a particular brain surgeon was unavailable.

I had been eavesdropping. I was sure it related to me. I was called in. I started, 'Milton, I was listening and I know I need brain surgery.'

'I was talking about somebody else. It was not you.'

'Come on, Milton, you know it was me.'

'It wasn't.'

'Are you sure?'

'I'm positive.'

'How do you know?' I said. 'Might it be for me?' On and on I went.

I remember being abroad. I paid about forty pounds to a doctor to come to my home and examine my earlobe. 'Does it have cancer?', 'Is cancer of the earlobe common?', 'Are you sure?', 'Are you sure you're sure?', 'I know you say you have never heard of such a thing, but might this be the first?', 'Are you sure?', 'If not the first, might this be the second?' On and on until he decided I'd had my forty pounds' worth.

Milton eventually said to me one day, when I asked if this would ever end, 'Yes – when you get bored with it.' And, in the end, I did. I had no recollection of any reason I did. But this constant introspection was exhausting. Suddenly the gloom and smog lifted and, thank G-d, has not returned.

Living in the moment is the only thing that makes sense – and not merely living on a work treadmill. One of the reasons is that – unless we are Winston Churchill, Gandhi or Homer Simpson – nobody will ultimately remember who we are anyway. This fact should help us with a work/life balance.

Working is like smoking. Although I have truly loved my work, I also loved smoking, but you finally realise that they are both dependency-creating habits. The only thing that makes you want a cigarette is the last one. The only thing that makes you want another case is the last one. The people who keep you sane are the ones you love and who love you.

Strangely enough, during my depressive episode – which I believe lasted fifteen months – I was able to work, in court, unaffected by what was going on outside. Work can bring on anxiety but it can also, as in my case, relieve one from it. I am acutely aware that, like any other addiction, and like Arnie Schwarzenegger, it can return.

When I took up my post at Luton Crown Court as a Judge, they introduced there an in-house psychiatric nursing team. It proved absolutely invaluable. How can a Judge really know whether, for instance, a Defendant has a personality disorder (and which of us doesn't!) and whether there are real questions over his mental fitness to be tried? This team were there to point us in the right direction and, if funds are not an issue, should be used in all courts.

Sometimes Marvellous Matron – a long-standing character at the Old Bailey, with her ever-ready paracetamol and Band-Aid, was just not enough.

46.

Art for art's sake

And finally on this topic, mindfulness and the need to find a balance in life.

One trick for achieving a work/life balance and sanity, includes having a totally distracting hobby – the sort of thing that skiing and sailing accomplish. But whilst I am a pre-ski and *après*-ski specialist, and have an elementary RYA dinghy certificate, neither of these did it for me. Painting does.

Art has always played a big, and increasingly bigger, part in my life. We are talking Sistine Chapel big. As a heart-on-the-sleeve type, the wonderful work of Rembrandt and Michelangelo give me the collie-wobbles, and my encounters with artists have been special and, strangely enough, law related.

Tom Keating has been described as the master forger of the twentieth century. I tracked him down to a tea shop in Dedham, Essex. He was a fine painter, but his skills soon persuaded him his career would be better served by forgeries rather than originals. His speciality was Samuel Palmers. He could hardly claim that he came across this skill accidentally; after all, if his pictures did not appear old enough he just popped a worthless Keating in the oven at gas mark four and, after it had wrinkled and cracked, out popped an old Palmer worth £40,000. These skills led to his trial at the Old Bailey for forgery.

He later told me about his trial, as did his co-Defendant, an antiques dealer who had a shop in Thaxted. They found the Judge to be not the least bit kindly. The dealer, who lived round the corner from me, managed to be acquitted. He told me that after this acquittal he went to dinner in a well-known Essex restaurant. He sent a drink over to an austere-looking man sitting at a table. The man raised and drank from the glass. A moment or two later, he came over saying, 'Do I know you'?

Came the answer, 'You should, you have been fxxking trying me for the last six weeks.'

BRINGING HOME THE BACON

Max Hill QC is the current Director of Public Prosecutions, and was head of chambers that had offered me a seat in 1984. As I worked out that I was likely to achieve all I could at the set I was in, I decided not to make a move, even though many of my friends were over there and I am sure I would have been happy.

I realise a lot of these overlaps can sound strange. How is it I could be on opposite sides of a case involving someone I was in chambers with? There again, how was it that I could lead a junior member of another set of chambers? What about the Inns of Court? How can a set of chambers be in one Inn's location and I be a member of another? What is the capital of Uruguay?

I'm tempted to explain. But as it is a matter of complete tedium to you and indifference to me, I shan't bother. Be satisfied with the fact that, despite Max's eminence, I ended up leading him in a case.

The case we did together was an Inland Revenue prosecution, which sounds boring enough but was enlivened by the fact that our client was related to the lover of the great artist Francis Bacon.

Max and I both fancy ourselves as luvvies: Max in theatre, me in art. Whilst I enjoy painting and, these days, spend a lot of time immersed in oil or acrylic, Max has every right to claim he is a thespian. His wife is also an actress (sorry, but I can't say 'actor'). In any event, we both found the idea of representing someone close enough to have breathed in Francis Bacon's genius exciting.

In the same way that Toulouse-Lautrec, visiting Montmartre for his absinthe, paid with a sketch of a can-can scene, I daydreamed of being paid by our client with an original piece by Francis Bacon. Had I been able to bring home the Bacon, I need never have worked again, I thought. I suppose I should have worked out that if our client was generous enough to reward us with a Bacon, he would have paid his income tax in the first place.

It is said we are never more than six steps away from being linked to Kevin Bacon. In this case, I was never more than two steps away from Francis Bacon. The opportunity presented itself again in 1998.

Whilst visiting Kenwood House, I saw there a Bacon for sale with a price tag of £1 million. To repeat a well-worn phrase, I took the opportunity to miss an opportunity. Rather than ring up some extremely rich mates and get each to chip in, of course I let it go by. This was one of his series featuring popes. It next came onto the market at £24 million, and after that at £64 million. Fortunately, when I read the last piece of news I was standing close to a wall which I could headbutt at 30mph in frustration.

But although Max and I were not offered a Bacon, not even a little one, we did sample the delights of something else. Golf is a frequent hobby for barristers, and Max and I gave it a spin. Having left the court at Snaresbrook early we would go into Epping Forest, to High Beech Pitch and Putt course to play nine holes. It was not St Andrews, but I doubt St Andrews does a hot chocolate and Wagon Wheels.

DOWN ON THE CANVAS

Over the last few years, I have constantly painted. I had first met a painting barrister in the guise of Andre de Moller, and very good at it he was. One of the sheikhs of somewhere or sultans of somewhere else paid him four hundred pounds an hour to fly wherever and paint a picture of whatever else. Naturally – at a much reduced rate – I offered to clean his brushes.

I was reintroduced to art whilst on holiday in South America. It was raining hard and we were stuck indoors. The hotel offered an hour's introduction to painting. After that hour, I spent about six hours a week painting for the next three years, first in acrylic and then oils. I give away everything I paint – whether people want it or not.

We need in our lives these things that stop rumination and introspection. If they are totally engrossing, do them. Is our art the window to our souls? Very possibly. I went once to the home of the solicitor acting for Ronnie and Reggie Kray, leaders of the East End underworld. He had an original Ronnie on his wall. It was a house painted as a square for the building and a triangle for a roof. It had four little oblongs for windows, with blood-red crosses in them for the lead that held the glass. I don't know how long the painting had been there, but left another ten minutes it would have congealed.

PART 10

Double-takes

47.

Take 1 – taking on the government

I seemed to need to be the chairman of everything.

At Chelmsford Tech, 'Oh, I'll chair the law society.'

Essex needs a Bar Mess Junior (Chairman), 'Oh, I'll do that.'

Essex needs a Bar Mess Senior, 'Oh, I'll do that.'

But whilst I am happy to deprecate my ambition, I do want to say that, once I secure such a position, I will do everything in my power to create a good and kind regime. The secret? Just keep smiling. Eventually people realise you are either a decent person or have lockjaw.

The Criminal Bar Association needs a Chairman: 'Oh, I'll do that.' And I did, and it represented my two most worthwhile years at the Bar.

As we experienced lockdown, the Bar found itself under pressure in exactly the way it did in 2013–14. It is one thing not to do something for the money, but it is quite another not to have the money to do the thing. Young barristers and solicitors found themselves constantly under attack. Lawyers are an easy target. Who likes them? More importantly, who would feel sorry for them? The government squeeze and squeeze until it hurts. The attacks came in a multitude of ways.

The schemes were just insulting. No pay for day two of a trial, we'll include it in day one. No fee for travelling to a conference to some remote prison. Why not? Ask your plumber on a two-day job to do the second for nothing, see what he says. Scythe down fees for small hearings. A day in court, travelling, waiting to get on, applying for somebody's liberty – £46.

On top of all of this came a further proposed series of cuts. The words 'straw' and 'camel's back' came to mind. The Ministry of Justice had come up with a scheme to continue cutting lawyers' fees. Instead of wage rises in line with inflation, they got wage cuts in excess of inflation. What was the reasoning behind this? The ethos was to constantly cut costs regardless of the fact that, in a democracy, an independent justice system is a necessity, along with a national health system and an education system – and it can't be done on the cheap.

The governments of the day disagreed: not only should law be done on the cheap, it does not even have to be done by people who know what they are doing. That went for those at the top of the ministerial tree, too.

Up until the 1970s, the Head of the Legal System, the Lord Chancellor, was a prominent lawyer. He knew how the system worked. But the process was changed. The Lord Chancellor's role merged with the

Minister of Justice. As I began to Chair the CBA the Minister of Justice in my day had no background in law, or none worth mentioning. Mr Christopher Grayling MP took over the job. He moved from the Ministry of Transport to Minister of Justice. I venture to suggest he knew more about the number 11 bus route that passed outside the Royal Courts of Justice than he did as to what went on inside.

By 2014 the Bar had begun to get vocal and political. Dissatisfaction was at its height. I was not political, and agree by and large that barristers and Judges should not be. But successive governments had stripped away the assets of the Criminal Justice system by regularly denuding the payment of the Bar. One day in 2013, about a day before the closing date for the election, I was approached and asked if I would consider standing for the Criminal Bar Association chairmanship. I happily agreed to, and was duly returned.

Earnings of a junior Barrister were down to the bone, and were barely better than minimum wage. This side of 'the Pond', a junior doctor after six years of training and three in practice may not be earning as much as £40,000 a year. At the Bar these rates, whilst comparable for a barrister aged thirty or more, are made worse by custom. Payment of overheads such as rent and expenses to chambers (shared work space) is one thing, but not all chambers are up to date. Historically, clerks were paid a percentage of earnings (far more than a generous salary), and there are still chambers where this is the case: a percentage of the combined fees earned by, say, 100 barristers is far more than the individuals themselves could earn. Of course, this is ridiculous, but where self-interest is at work it is difficult to change the system. The aim of the barrister once in a boat will be not to rock it. And so those benefitting, of course, will do anything to make sure the boat does not sink. It leaves many in the profession struggling to keep their heads above water and carrying big debt.

That said, as in all professions, at the other end were people of fortunately high earnings. I was one of those, and knew I would have that pointed out to me in any negotiations I undertook as Chair of the CBA. I always responded that it was precisely because I was in that position that I was able to take time out to represent the younger members who would make up the future of the profession. I chose a pithy slogan: rather than 'Not a penny less' I went for 'Not a penny more' (i.e. no more cuts for the Criminal Bar would be acceptable).

I began to write a blog. I did not call it a blog, as I did not know what a blog was. But my ardent predecessor had produced a 'Monday Message' to distribute to the troops. His slogan had been 'Do right, fear no one' – a wonderful maxim. But I knew that the only thing that would achieve a better deal was either a strike or the threat of a strike, and gradually

I sowed the seed of such action in successive Monday Messages. They took up a lot of my weekends for that year – what with me drafting them and my wife translating them into English.

My predecessor, Mike Turner QC, and I were very different. He came from a set of chambers renowned for its left-wing views, whilst I – until recently – had preferred that partisan politics should play no part in the administration of justice. Mike thought I would need my sinews stiffening, and suggested that Tony Cross QC, a northern terrier, would make a good partner as vice-chairman. Tony was exceptional. Fearlessness is contagious, and together with our wonderful committee – Chris Henley, Richard Bentwood and Emma Wood, to name but a very few – we girded our loins for what was to follow. Our administrator, Aaron Dolan, organised the girding.

Mike had made it clear that he would not meet with the Lord Chancellor, and the feeling was reciprocated. I thought it better to meet, look him in the eye and tell him of our resolve. Each week the Monday Message went out to everyone, and I mean everyone: the Bar, solicitors, Judges and government. To the Ministry of Justice, it became an Enigma machine – albeit one without a code. They still felt they needed to crack it – and those who wrote with it.

Ultimately, like Popeye, I cracked open the spinach and proclaimed: 'I've had all I can stands and I can't stands no more.'

It was my view that, to be taken seriously, government had to understand that we would take them on, and if they threatened to cut our fees further we would strike. In successive messages, I announced that we would strike first for half a day, next a whole day, then two days and ultimately indefinitely.

The enormity of this as a symbol was clear. The Bar had never walked out on strike in its 400-year history. This was a conservative profession. A strike was coupled with an additional weapon. If a barrister cannot do a trial – if, for instance, he or she is over-running – it will be handed over to another. This is called a 'return'. If each barrister subscribed to saying they would not do a return, the trial would be postponed until someone would become available. The effect would be catastrophic. People in prison have to be tried within a certain time, called Custody Time Limits (CTLs). If the time is exceeded they become eligible for release. The prospect of alleged murderers and rapists walking the streets was a real one.

During this time, I met regularly with the Minister of Justice. His lack of understanding of the system was fairly comprehensive. But it began to dawn on the ministry he headed that the system was about to fall apart.

The plans were to cut the legal aid bill by £220 million.

My plan was to show the government through incrementally increasing steps of protest that this would

not happen. We had the power to stop the courts operating, and if needs be that is what we would do.

In November 2013 came the opening skirmish.
National press and TV covered a demo we held
outside Lincoln's Inn, telling the government we were
one month away from industrial action.

Channel 4 picked up this sound bite: 'If the rally
doesn't work, then more drastic action has to be
taken. The Criminal Bar is not prepared to work in
the face of these cuts.'

The *Mirror* ran with, 'Legal aid cuts: murderers,
rapists and paedophiles could walk free, warns top
barrister.' (I liked the last two words.) We were not
Unite or Unison, but we did have four thousand very
angry members.

As the *Guardian* reported, on 6 January 2014 – for
the first time in history – we withdrew our labour. We
left court and congregated outside in wigs and gowns.
I made a speech outside Southwark Crown Court
whilst others spoke outside all other crown courts.

The *Sunday Times* covered 'My week' on 12 January, under the title 'I Rest My Case on Behalf of
Pauper of the Bailey, M'Lud'. The sub-paragraphs
of the article I was responsible for read: 'Making a
stand', 'I'll eat my wig' and 'All work no pay'. One of
the paragraphs the newspaper inserted was entitled,
'Handbags at dawn', a reference to two of our protesters carrying designer handbags, a mistake our PR
firm did not let us repeat.

This was not just about individual lawyers' fees. The direct consequences of the cuts would be an impact on diversity, as only the wealthy would be able to afford to enter the profession. These cuts would put access to the profession back fifty years.

We had powerful friends, and the way to keep them on board was to keep them informed: I went weekly to see the Recorder of London (top dog at the Old Bailey, who had himself been Chairman of the CBA), as well as the then Lord Chief Justice John Thomas, top dog of everything. All were charming, all quietly supportive. I also met with the Lord Chancellor Chris Grayling weekly at the Ministry of Justice, quietly assuring him that what I said we would do, we would do. The first protests would happen on a Saturday – outside of court time – the second on a half-a-day in court time and, thereafter, he could look forward to a whole day, then two days and even unto eternity.

On 8 March came the second day of protest. This was in Parliament Square. Inflatable Graylings of a size that would have stopped the Luftwaffe were flown and speeches delivered to aid the Bar. I shared a platform with Gerry Conlon of the Guildford Four. (Until then I thought the Guildford Four included Daniel Day-Lewis.)

Publicity was enormous. All the daily newspapers ran with the items whilst radio and TV ran interviews. On the day of the strike, our cause was carried on all the main TV and radio networks, from John Humphrys on Radio 4 to me sharing a sofa with Eamonn Holmes – albeit together; it was a tight squeeze. I was met, as predicted, with the question, 'How do you have the cheek to claim the Bar was underpaid, when one only had to look at your earnings?' The answer was easy; just because Humphrys was one of the highest earners on radio did not mean young journalists could not feel aggrieved, and as time would tell, this did not mean women should be treated unequally, nor that Humphrys should not espouse their cause.

We went from Three Counties Radio to Radio Moscow. What would happen with the rule of law? Radio Moscow offered a dacha on a lake outside Moscow for an exclusive interview. Three Counties Radio offered me a tour of inspection at an artificial insemination yard featuring Bedford's prize bull. In reality, both interviews occurred outside Chancery Lane tube station.

My message was the same. After all chambers' overheads, such as rent and expenses of travel and the like, the poor rates of pay meant youngsters could not come to the Bar, turning it back into the home for the elite that it had been for so long. The media tended not to believe the extremity of the plight, but a rate of £46 for a day's work before overheads and expenses was no joke. We were wearing everyone down.

Meetings with Mr Grayling became ever more frequent, until one day we were summoned by his PA and the Chief Exec of the MoJ and, as our mouths dropped open, we were told that the government was rescinding its proposed cuts to the Bar.

Having been offered what we asked for, saying 'Yes' was not as simple as you would think it would be. Along with the Battle of the Bar was the war for the solicitors. They too were being squeezed, and their firms being put in jeopardy. Our approach had been united. But Mr Grayling came to me with an offer only for the Bar. I was the Chairman of the CBA; the Law Society had their own leaders.

I put the question, as to whether we should take the victory or hang out for the solicitors as well, to a ballot of the membership of the Criminal Bar. A strong majority said take the win. We were about to become one of the few bodies to stop a government in its tracks.

How did we do it? By the steely resolve of the vast majority of the profession to down tools when we did and not to take up the work that was not being done.

As always in life, people came to me to say, whatever the sacrifice, 'How can I help?' But some would ring me saying, 'Oh, I have this case ...' and it was truly an inquiry about how they could improve their own positions. Mr Grayling even set up a new body called the Public Defender Service as a way to employ barristers at a cheaper rate and cut the legs from under us. The Bar did not forgive them.

When everything quietened down, one of the government civil servants asked, 'What should we do with them?'

'Sack them,' I suggested.

THAT'S ANOTHER FINE MESS YOU'VE GOTTEN US INTO

In 2019, the government devised another silly scheme.

You would have thought that the optimum system required a number of courts operating per building, each manned by one Judge on a daily basis to get through the backlog of criminal cases.

No. Too easy. Notwithstanding a backlog in cases waiting to be heard, the Ministry of Justice cut the number of 'sitting days' available, so that Judges had to find other things to do rather than sit every day.

For example, if a month was, for argument's sake, four weeks long, that should make twenty sitting days for each of the courts in the building. If you had six courts, that would make for 120 sitting days. Right? Wrong.

It was decided to allow that court building to sit, say 100 days. Why? And how would the days be allocated? What money would be saved? The building had to be paid for, along with the staff. The Judges were on fixed salaries. Where were these great savings to be found? The answer was this. The government were up to their tricks again: fewer cases meant fewer advocates' fees. Once again, the barrister and solicitor advocates were in the front line for cuts. And having come out on strike in 2014, it looked like in 2019 nothing had been learned. Remember the old unattributed saying, 'Those who do not learn history are doomed to repeat it.'

So cutting court-sitting days was a foolish idea that became exacerbated by Covid, which meant even if the courts wanted to, they could not open.

But in cutting court days there was nothing new in it appearing nonsensical and counterintuitive. During my forty years in the profession, so many pilot schemes introduced had failed and been withdrawn, and every cost-saving scheme has merely cost money and engendered lower and lower morale.

There had been a pilot scheme to split sitting hours in courts. For instance, 8 a.m. to 1 p.m. would be spent doing criminal cases, 2 p.m. to 7 p.m. doing other cases. How were prisoners to arrive for 7 a.m to see counsel? By leaving prison at 4 a.m. on the prison bus? How was a young, married barrister to arrive at court for 7 a.m.? Leave their young child abandoned until the chip shop opened, as happened in my grandfather's day?

48.

Take 2 – taking the Queen's shilling

Or, why I became a Judge. Good question. Answers, please, on a postcard.

Like many other decisions in my life, I believe it was made by default. As I approached sixty-five, I was confronted with a number of options. The advantages of staying at the Bar were clear. Despite the nature of the job and, like an actor never knowing where my next job will come from, I felt comfortable. I had managed to carve out a reputation as fearless in how I fought for the client and stood up to those Judges who seemed to want to spend their time being unpleasant. The money remained attractive at the upper end of the job, whereas the Queen's Shilling had been largely devalued since the days of King Henry VIII and, of course, now was only worth 5p.

What were the choices?

Choice number 1: Stay at the Bar.

Choice number 2: Retire. I loved public-speaking engagements, I was doing a lot of work for charity and we could travel/experience a new culture, make new friends.

Choice number 3: Do something new. I answered an advertisement. In 2016 there was a regular announcement of a recruitment process for Judges. It would involve form-filling, referee-providing and an interview. In other words, a competition. The last time I had won a competition was when I suggested to the *TV Comic* that Fred Flintstone's wife, Wilma, could use an empty oyster shell as a purse. I won two tickets to Bertram Mills' Circus. I was aged sixty-four (not when I won the tickets). And the last time I had held down a regular job was at Woolworths in Leytonstone. I was paid about eight pounds a week, aged fifteen. I was a socialist when it came to fruit and veg. As people came to the vegetable part of the store, I would assess their wealth. If they were old and infirm and asked for two pounds of potatoes they would get ten potatoes. If they came to Woolworths in a taxi that waited outside and asked for two pounds of potatoes, they got three potatoes. Woolworths was sited near the bowling alley and Wimpy bar, where I had had mixed fortunes. I once bought a new pair of hipsters (in those days I had hips). I had gone to put ketchup on my chips but, unfortunately, the leaf at the top of the squeezy plastic tomato was not secure, and red sauce ruined the trousers.

Back to the application: a number of people around me were strong supporters of option 3 – go for the job.

So, I thought, What the hell, I'll go in for the competition and make up my mind later.

I think that in the process I managed to show myself to have the legal knowledge of an orangutan and the intellectual agility of a tortoise. I also proved to the Judge and A.N. Other who interviewed me that I was totally incapable of making up my mind. But then this was about the only interview I'd ever had. I had good references from my life at the Bar, but the examination/interview process I've already said hadn't gone well. Whilst I was waiting for the result, I bumped into one of my highest-placed referees. Annoyingly, he thought I was bound to do OK, and if my performance had been poor, my referees would do the heavy lifting. 'I reckon you would only need, say 6/10 and you'll be fine.'

Me: 'Ohh …' I answered doubtfully.

Him: '5/10?'

Me: 'Ohh,' resignedly.

We settled on a 'four' as likely. Strangely enough, since the days when I sat an elocution examination at my preparatory school, I'd always managed to hit a four and, in my day, 40 per cent was a pass.

They offered me a job.

But where would they put me? The deciding factor to go for option 3 was that it would give me a change of lifestyle that I looked forward to. I did not think I would find the work difficult, and so it proved to be. I believed we would get to start a new half-life in Essex.

After all, I had gone to school in Essex; college in Essex; practised most of my life in Essex; been the Junior of the Bar Mess in Essex; leader of the Bar Mess in Essex; my friends were at the Bar and on the Bench in Essex. Where else would they send me?

Where did the Ministry of Justice send me to sit?

Obviously, Luton.

Luton in Bedfordshire. No point in tapping into forty years of goodwill and community relations, they thought, that would be sensible. I went and spoke to one of the Presiding Judges. He thought Luton was the obvious spot. Obvious to whom? And then 'they' complain morale is low amongst the judiciary.

When I was told Luton, I screamed, and I don't mean inwardly.

Strangely, I did have some tenuous links with the town. My granddad had been a GP there and Benny Hill delivered milk to my grandparents, hence his song 'Ernie (The Fastest Milkman in the West)' was based on an event in his life. It became an event in my life when myself and my friend Robert Levy QC, commercial Silk, did a duet of alternate verses from 'Ernie …' at his daughter's Bat Mitzvah. We thought it was great. She cried and said we had ruined her life. We had to explain it was not all about her.

No, I'm afraid sending me to Luton rather than Chelmsford says a lot about poor management. It also shows that I have a yellow streak of compliance down my back, which is why I accepted the location.

I took the job. And Luton Crown Court did turn out to be great. It was nothing to do with the judicial authorities. It was great because of the tradition of the Resident Judges there; Richard Foster, Barbara Mensah and the other Judges were a laid-back, marvellous group of people. Not a smidgeon of pomposity between them. I was very happy there.

Staff make all the difference and, if you are a talker, it makes life very pleasant. I'm a talker. I need to laugh and talk nonsense to people from the time I arrive until I leave.

RECORDER (PART-TIME JUDGE – NOT FLUTE)

Judging wasn't an entirely new experience for me. Since 1996, I had sat as first an Assistant Recorder and then a Recorder. Recorder is an Olde Worlde title for a part-time Judge.

Once appointed, you were supposed to sit for up to twenty days a year, which was later reduced to fifteen days. Now, I hear you readers spotting an anomaly. If they have reduced sitting days for full-time Judges what work is left for part-timers? Well spotted.

None. How will they get experience? Give up. And so it is that, latterly, the powers that be have, pretty well, cut sitting days entirely for Recorders.

I did much of my part-time sitting at the Old Bailey as a Recorder.

There were wonderful traditions at that court. For instance, one of the courts is a converted toilet, and the

Judges' changing room behind it is the size of a bidet. That is the court often provided to part-time Judges.

But prestige does its best to make up for it, and I enjoyed it. A few days sitting in Court no. 1 reminds you of the celebrated murder trials that had taken place in that courtroom. Most killings in history seem to have taken place in a bath. There was 'Brides in the Bath', the 'Brides in Sulphuric Acid in the Bath' and Dennis Nilsen cutting them up and storing them in the bath. My advice to you, if you want to live a long and happy life, is don't bathe. Especially if your boiler is on the blink.

I adjudicated over nothing so grand, but, that said, lunch was fun. The City Corporation that ran and paid for the court ran and paid for lunch. There was always good grub and good guests. Tradition had it that you would go into lunch fully robed.

I suppose if I had had a judicial career, rather than just the tail end of a barristerial one, I might have climbed higher, but lunch, fully robed, provided by the City of London Corporation in its banqueting room did not really compete with the £3.99 meal in Chopstix, Luton. In Chopstix, you did not have to wear robes, although for men, trousers were compulsory.

PART 11

Here come the Judges

49.

Judges, dead or alive

As a barrister, using a boxing metaphor, I was sure I was the slugger Mike Tyson rather than the butterfly Muhammad Ali.

But now I took on the referee's white shirt and bow tie.

More apposite, my new role, having exhausted my life at the Bar, was being like a Sumo wrestler who has run out of salt, and has opted for the Gyoji (Sumo ref) role.

As I have explained ad nauseam, I had spent forty-one years watching the horrors of what men did to one another, but I was about to sit in the umpire's chair. Whilst I'm sure I could remain neutral between Federer and Nadal, could I be equally impartial between prosecution and defence, or would I be infected by the jaundice against Defendants I have spoken of?

I have no doubt that one day I will make a fine adult. In a court building, each Judge has his own room – or chambers, as some still cling to saying. Many have things called books (remember them) lining shelves. Mine has model cars, soldiers and toys generally.

My Judicial career did not start well. At a Judicial seminar, the trainer and inspirational ex-Lord Chief Justice Igor Judge advised, 'Don't be stopped speeding on the way to court,' and I wasn't.

But my car was and, within six months of starting the job, I had points. Apparently, if you have more than six points on your licence you are supposed to report yourself to the Lord Chancellor's Office, though I can't see the point unless he is willing to take the points for you, but then he should keep in mind what I said about perverting the course of justice.

I said to myself I would do the job for the maximum of three years, but like all promises we make we lie and self-deceive. So I have passed the four-year mark and, as I now have a clean licence, I think I will quit whilst I'm ahead.

However ghastly coronavirus has been, individually and nationally, it has shown many that slowing the pace of life down brings enormous delights – easy for me to say, I know.

But having said that, the main reason one might choose to take the job of Crown Court Judge is because you closely touch the lives of ordinary people. You are involved with people in distress – as victims, Defendants and witnesses. If you went to the Bar to do good, you can have the same lofty ambition on the Bench.

You get to exercise and invoke calm in a turbulent world, and get to use your judgement in a fairly powerful way. You decide who will go to prison, who will not – and I assure you, the joy lies in those you might have sent to prison, but don't.

At St Albans (I moved there from Luton after eighteen months), one of my clerks, Tony, has me down to a tee. If we see that my afternoon list has two short matters in it, he will usually turn around to me and silently adopt the air of an officer's adjutant: 'I'll get the Jag warmed up and brought around the front, sir.'

How was I to behave on the Bench? From where should come my examples? I am afraid that, by and large, my reading of Judges through history, as well as my first-hand experience of them has taught me how *not* to behave rather than the opposite.

Judges, I suppose, tend to be divided into two camps:

TYRANTS AND PUSSY CATS

I mentioned the tradition of dining at the Inn. When I first went into dinner at the Inner Temple, that is where I saw my best-known examples of Judges. The first I mention was in a wheelchair but was not Ironside.

Even the sight of Lord Goddard at top table, at the Inner Temple, a million miles from us students, made you shudder. You were looking at an English institution. A 'hanging Judge' and known as such. He seemed as old as his predecessor, Judge Jeffreys, known as the hanging Judge of the Bloody Assizes, who had ordered the execution of the rebels who rose against James II. I am sure Lord Goddard would have done his best to equal that record given the chance. Jeffreys, too, was a member of the Inner Temple, the Inn in which I am a Governing Bencher – supposedly a higher part of its hierarchy.

Goddard had overseen the jurisprudential shambles that was Bentley and Craig. Two young men, Bentley, the older, and Craig, the younger, were effecting a burglary by climbing first onto the roof. As police chased them, the younger shot and killed one of them. The youth who had shot him could not in law be hanged, so he was sent to prison, whilst the adult Bentley, who had not fired the shot, but was deemed to have encouraged Craig, was hanged. (Remember joint enterprise.)

One of the controversies was whether Bentley had said, 'Let him have it, Chris,' to Craig, on one interpretation, thereby encouraging Craig the youth to kill a policeman. The other interpretation was that it might have meant, 'Surrender the gun'. It required the Jury to reject any ambivalence and return a verdict of murder. (In fact, Bentley denied saying it at all.) Lord Goddard did the rest. Black hat, death for Bentley. Additionally, as if a siren as to what was to come, Bentley was challenged by mental issues. One way or another, he clearly should never have hanged. Apart from seeing Goddard from afar, I never came before him. But afar was close enough for me.

A little closer came the second nightmare. Lord Justice 'Fred' Lawton. I did appear both before him

and alongside him. We were both invited to debate
the new test for causing death by dangerous driving
for Central TV in Birmingham.

Research online reveals, 'Lawton had joined the
British Union of Fascists and founded the Cambridge
University Fascist Association. In 1936 he was
adopted as the fascist candidate for Hammersmith
North, but did not contest the seat owing to the post-
ponement of the 1940 general election due to World
War II. He later defended many a fascist.' Simply
put, his history contained the word 'fascist' too often
to infer strong left-wing, libertarian tendencies.
Here, life had some symmetry. One of the few briefs
I rejected was to defend the leader of the National
Front, the forerunner to the British National Party –
for some public nuisance on the south coast.

Anyway, Fred Lawton, by the time I appeared in
Central's studios with him, was arguing on the same
side as me, that the consequences of death by dangerous driving – i.e. the death – must be given more
prominence in the sentencing process.

Melford Stevenson is exhibit no. 3 in the horror
show of Judges.

Sir Robin Dunn described him as 'the worst judge
since the war'. But that no doubt was subjective. In
1955, he defended Ruth Ellis against the charge of
murdering her lover. Stevenson's decision to keep his
cross-examination of the prosecution witnesses to a
minimum and his 'near silent performance in court'

have been severely criticised. He opened the defence by saying, 'Let me make this abundantly plain: there is no question here but this woman shot this man … you will not hear one word from me – or from the lady herself – questioning that.' While a defence was put, the Jury took twenty-three minutes to find Ellis guilty; she was sentenced to be hanged and was the last woman executed in the UK. I believe that today this would be known as rubbish advocacy.

In 1969 he sentenced the Kray Twins, Reggie and Ronnie, to a minimum of thirty years in jail each, saying, 'In my view, society has earned a rest from your activities.' He remarked later that the Krays had only told the truth rarely during the trial – once was when Reggie referred to a barrister as 'a fat slob'. Clearly a Judge not averse to a bit of spite.

When I look back at this rogues' gallery of Judges, I do so in a way that many of the elders of my profession would disapprove. But it must be clear that I set them out in this way as they appear in no way to portray mercy, compassion or kindness. To the contrary, they appear cold and cruel.

I know I called this section 'Tyrants and pussy cats' but have not named any pussy cats. Is it a worrying feature of life if we remember the worst rather than the best?

50.

On your broomstick

Essex did have at least one judicial feline, though he dressed in judicial robes that in reality were a wolf's clothing.

I mention Melford, as one of the Judges most affecting my career worshipped him. His Honour Judge Peter Greenwood liked to think he modelled himself on him in terms of prestige and an ability to instill fear in all who came before him. In fact, Peter had a much softer and warmer underbelly than Stevenson. Greenwood ruled the roost at Chelmsford for twenty-five years. At first, we had a hate-hate relationship and next a love-hate relationship and finally a qualified love-qualified love relationship.

I am afraid there is no point avoiding the fact that he could be a snob and could be a bully; none the worse for that, I hear you say. I guess it's a variant on the Stockholm syndrome that made us – I hope it's not too far off the mark – fond of each other. He knew I would do everything legitimately in my power to defend my client to the nth degree, and I knew he had the Judge's start point of antipathy for Defendants.

His view was that if people were innocent they would not have been charged. There were very many idiosyncratic meetings. Once, when I wanted to ask a policeman about the fact that he had failed a police exam, the Judge asked me to come to his room.

'How on earth is that relevant?' he asked.

'Well, I'm challenging the officer's accuracy of note-taking, so his exam failings are relevant.' It was a thin argument. It was actually a rubbish argument, of which maturity would have made me think better. The Judge's response was to say I had better mention the question of my client's bail later; in other words, if I insisted in going down this line, my client was likely to be banged up overnight. Anyway, I did, and he was!

But appearing regularly before the same Judge brought some great moments.

I had a client who burgled a house in Bocking, outside of Braintree.

'If I'm not mistaken they are four-bedroom executive homes,' said the Judge.

'I wouldn't know,' answered the Defendant. 'I'm a burglar, not an effing estate agent.'

After his death I was pleased to read that one of my cases remained lodged in his memory. I prosecuted a conspiracy to murder. As often happens in the law, rather than going through a messy divorce, murder seems simpler and more attractive. I assume that is because whilst for murder you will spend over twenty years in prison, at least apart from fraud, you don't have to give away your assets.

This particular Defendant did try numerous alternative routes to separation, none of which worked. He even brought in a Welsh wizard to apply a hex to her. I decided to call the wizard to give evidence for the Crown of the Defendant's intent. The Judge's son later told the press in an obituary to his father:

'Dad, having heard this man's evidence, and finding it totally irrelevant, sent him packing out of court with the words, "The sooner you hop on your broomstick and fly back to Bristol, the better."'

Judge Greenwood was an object of terror not only amongst wayward priests, the criminal fraternity and old lags but also to young barristers. He was no soft touch, and anyone committing a burglary in Essex knew they would be going to prison for four years if caught. (It is an interesting principle of sentencing as a deterrent, that, as a burglar has his jemmy out and aligned with the hinges on your back gate, through his mind would pass Judge Greenwood's face and the assurance of four years.)

What I must truly commend Judge Greenwood for was actually acting out the old music hall routine with me.

Judge: 'I am not prepared to let the Jury hear that evidence.'

Defendant from the Dock: 'Fxxk off, Judge.'

Judge: 'Mr Lithman. What did your client say?'

Me: 'Fxxk off, Judge.'

Judge: 'I was only asking.'

Just as Judges themselves are complex beings, so are the relationships between Bench and Bar.

Another of Essex's Judges, instilled with a natural disinclination towards believing a Defendant was capable of being innocent, was Judge Brian Watling. He was a man of the cloth, and thus a force to be reckoned with. He wished he could include fire and brimstone in his sentencing. Considering Oliver Cromwell slaughtered the populations of Drogheda and Wexford in the name of Heaven, Judges with a religious bent likewise bring with them onto the Bench the wrath of the Lord, and although Watling never ordered the decimation of the people of Clacton, he was a tough man. On occasion, he would send me handwritten notes complimenting me on a particular cross-examination I had performed, and I had affection for him, but if the truth is here to be told – and I see no reason why it should not be – we must add the late Reverend Watling to the list of Judges from whom I learned, and not in an entirely good way.

As you may know, a Judge will note a witness's evidence supposedly fully and impartially. But, from time to time, 'Watters' would note a particularly good piece of evidence for the prosecution and then deliberately pick up his highlighting pen and heavily underline it, looking at the Jury as he did it as if to say, 'There you go, members of the Jury, he'll never wriggle out of that one.' Needless to say, that is far from proper judicial behaviour. The function of a Judge should be to present an impartial summary of the facts in an impartial way. I remember at one time finding myself on the Bench and looking momentarily at the Jury. I instantly shouted internally, 'Nigel, who do you think you are? Judge Watling?'

51.

Judge John Deed

Judges in court are not my only experience with Judges. I once worked on the TV set of a fictional Judge. I learned that Judge John Deed was no better a role model as Judge than the real thing.

On a blustery Monday morning, a friend of a friend contacted me to see if I was available to act as the legal adviser on the TV crime drama, *Judge John Deed*. This was usually the gig of David Etherington QC, without doubt the finest raconteur I have ever met. The TV show starred the actors Martin Shaw and Jenny Seagrove.

Martin Shaw was best known for his role in the cops and robbers TV show *The Professionals*. Jenny Seagrove could be mistaken for Jenny Agutter, except that Ms Seagrove tended always to act with her kit on, whilst Ms Agutar was no stranger to goosebumps.

Also, unlike Ms Agutter, she was well known for a long relationship with the *Times* restaurant critic who wrote the weekly column 'Winner's Dinner', Michael Winner. Of Michael Winner the joke ran: which was the best table in a restaurant? Answer: The one furthest from Michael Winner. He also did

a well-known advert for an insurance company that
merely required him to repeatedly lisp 'Take it easy,
my dear' in a horrid manner.

I turned up at the abandoned school building in
Hertfordshire where this was being filmed. First, we
cleared up the question of the fee for my attendance.
The film production answered my gentle eenquiry as
to how much they had in mind for my professional
service by saying, 'We had in mind nothing.' As previously mentioned, this did not mean 'we have nothing
in mind,' but rather 'we propose to pay you nothing.'
I thought this was a reasonable assessment of the
quality of my services, and waited by the coffee van
to be called on.

It was explained that what was expected was that I
would be told of the scenario for the day in court, and
I was there to ensure it had reality. It soon became
clear that there was no interest in my view of the plot,
although, at one point, as they were short-handed, I
did manage to secure a small but not insignificant
walk-on part – opening a door and closing it behind
me. That evening, I boasted that I felt I had opened
that door with a style and grace never equalled in all
the annals of door opening (and closing).

Judge John Deed took his place in the mythical
court to hear an application for an injunction made
by mythical barrister Ms Seagrove. This was at
10.30 a.m. At midday he invited her to his mythical chambers behind his mythical court and seduced

her. At 2 p.m. all of the parties came into court to hear the result of the 10.30 a.m. application. Judge John Deed announced that barrister Ms Seagrove had lost her application. At the end of the day, over a cup of tea, Martin Shaw asked me what I'd thought of the day's work. I told him that the idea you would hear from a barrister at 10.30, have sex with her at 12 noon and then find against her at 2 p.m., was a little unlikely.

But as to the actual legal proceedings I thought you all had your wigs on straight.

Martin Shaw and Jenny Seagrove were delightful.

I was to see Ms Seagrove again.

She contacted me and said that the script required her to become a part-time Judge, a Recorder. She said she had seen from my CV that I too was a Recorder, sitting therefore as a part-time Judge for about fifteen days a year. She said she wanted to know what it was like. As opposed to my customary fee, nothing, I said it would be nice to tell her this over lunch at the Savoy Hotel. As I was providing the advice it was only fair I chose the venue. As we sat down, I said that in return for telling her about being a Recorder, I wanted to know what it was like to go out with Michael Winner. We agreed.

During my omelette and chips (probably called *omelete et chips* in the Savoy), I told her some of the things about being a Recorder. For instance, you wore your everyday barrister's robes and didn't let senior counsel take liberties, otherwise the gig is much the same as with an ordinary Judge.

In exchange, she shared, amongst others, this tale: Michael Winner would take them for dinner, at the end of which he would light up a cigar. When the staff asked him to extinguish it, he insisted on standing up and asking all the other diners to vote as to whether they minded or not. He lost that vote 47–0. Ultimately, he also lost Jenny Seagrove. I am afraid discretion does not allow me to share more of what she told me.

52.

Judge-itis

I first became acquainted with an -itis by warnings from my mother. If I did not brush my teeth and clean my gums, I would contract gingivitis, one of the first signs of gum disease. She also added that all of my teeth would fall out. That did concern me, as I was not quite sure how with no teeth I would be able to negotiate my way around a Bounty bar or, even more troubling, a Walnut Whip, in which the walnut was the prize at both the top and bottom of a chocolate whirl.

'Itis' is a suffix used in pathological terms that denotes inflammation of an organ (bronchitis, gastritis, neuritis). In a Judge, the organ that it attacks is his ego, with particular regard to his view of his own importance. He believes that in practice he should have been more successful and upon appointment insufficient regard was paid to his brilliance. For these oversights by fate, somebody has to pay the price. That price is to be as unpleasant as he can to advocates who come before him and whom he believes will not stand up to him.

Before continuing, let me make it clear that Judge-itis is not a legal pandemic. The number of sufferers are relatively and thankfully few, albeit that, in distinction to pandemics, masks and two metres distance will not help keep them at bay. They harangue and shout and bully and pay no heed whatever to the difficulties that already face the advocate.

They wish cases to be completed at breakneck speed, whatever the cost, and woe betide an advocate who might want to leave court early to attend to domestic issues or toothache. They fail to grasp the fact that however quickly this bus arrives and departs there is another right behind.

In considering Judge-itis, some questions arise:

When does it first occur? By definition, the usual rule is that you cannot contract Judge-itis unless and until you are appointed as a Judge. However, of a certain Judge I knew, it was maintained that he had Judge-itis from the time he was a pupil, in other words when he was a mere snip of a lad whose career was in its infancy. As so often in these cases, this Judge had two characters: Judge Jekyll and Judge Hyde, with a switch to control which face you saw.

A young barrister coming before Judge Hyde has a sense of dread and foreboding that his day is about to be awful. He is rarely disappointed.

And that is the harm in Judge-itis: it makes the professional life of those who come before the sufferers miserable. Those Judges believe the courtroom must revolve around them. They will ignore the fact that the Defendant is manipulating or pulling the advocate in a particular direction. Whatever the strength of the prosecution's case, he has the right to plead Not Guilty and, if the Judge believes that he is paying no regard to the strength of the Crown's case, being rude to counsel will not change that.

That is not to say that, from time to time, a Judge will find his patience being stretched to beyond reason and, equally, an advocate find a Judge at a particular time unhelpful in his interruptions. But that is not Judge-itis, that is just life in a fraught situation.

Where does it come from? It is often contracted by those who not only had an indifferent career as a lawyer in practice, but who went on to get a job in the judiciary that they believe is beneath their brilliance and more important their dignity.

Every Crown Court Judge with Judge-itis believes he should have been a High Court Judge or at the very least an Old Bailey Judge. He does not pause to think that maybe, like water, nature helps him find his own level. Most Judges with Judge-itis have so many chips on their shoulders that they could have been manufactured by McCain.

What are its symptoms? First is the temptation that certain Judges find irresistible, to shout at those that appear before them. In front of one Judge at Southwark, I was always tempted to look around me when he spoke. Had he asked why, I would have replied that I was certain that there must be a dog in the courtroom. Not that anyone would speak to a dog the way he barked at people. He once told me in the middle of a submission to 'sit down'. I explained calmly that after eighteen years as one of Her Majesty's Counsel he could safely assume that I knew when I should sit and when I should stand. This was a moment for standing, and I would continue to stand until it was time to sit.

A clear sign that the Judge is afflicted is demonstrated in his urge to arrange for cases to begin and end at the most inconvenient times for counsel. For example, if you sit as a Judge in Suffolk or Norfolk, telling counsel you require them in court at 9.30 means that unless they pitch a tent by the side of the courthouse, they may well have to leave home at between 5.30 and 6.30 to arrive at court by 9.15 in order to earn a paltry sum for their attendance.

It would not occur to the Judge that the kind and appropriate thing might be to consider starting at between 10 a.m. and 10.30 a.m. In the 'old days' courts started at 10.30 and finished at around 4 p.m. – for good reason. It meant that one could arrive at court at 9 a.m. to meet with the client, obtain their daily instructions on the evidence and prepare them for the ordeal ahead. At the end of the court day, there would be another conference with the client before returning to chambers to prepare for the next day's hearing and attend to the rest of one's professional life, leaving what little remained for a private life.

Next, court listing.

Determining the date when a case will begin is generally done by administrators aptly known as listing officers. Juggling all of these balls is an art rather than a science. Debbie Downer at Luton was one such artist, although not all administrators have her skills.

However, one of the roles sometimes exercised by Judges, and performed by those with Judge-itis with glee, is to allocate a date for upcoming trials. Common sense dictates that this should aim for the swift coming to trial for the case, and at the same time recognise the convenience of all the parties. In other words, the Defendants, the Complainants, the witnesses, and the lawyers, to name but a few, albeit not necessarily in that order.

The Judge laid low by Judge-itis will give no regard to convenience of the advocates, in fact exactly the opposite. A Judge can boost his sense of power by listing the trial for a date that will mean the advocate must cancel a long-booked family holiday, and require them to choose between their practice and their marriage, admittedly not a simple choice in every case.

There are varying degrees of severity. Most are never touched by it. Some have a mild form. Occasionally there is full-blown Judge-itis. In common with other parts of life, those occupying the lower parts of the food chain are the quickest to be difficult and officious, whilst those with nothing to prove and happy in their own skins have time and patience for everyone.

For instance, I was once mid-case when I had to attend the Court of Appeal at short notice. Convention has it that the Crown Court Judge adjourns his case to let the advocate go to the court of higher jurisdiction. The Judge I was before huffed and puffed, desperately out of sorts that his case had to give way. 'Well, I want you back ready to resume at twelve noon,' he demanded. As the case was in Northampton, allowing for the fact that the appeal in London was listed at 10.30, I could only get back on time if the appeal scheduled to last 1.5 hours in fact only lasted seven seconds.

What actually happened was that the Lord Chief Justice Almighty, who had got wind of this, telephoned Judge Tin Pot to tell him I would be back for 2 p.m. and that was that.

The other instance that stands out in my mind was during Cheltenham race week. Some Crown Courts have visiting High Court Judges spending time there, often to try controversial high-profile cases – baby murders, etc. During the Cheltenham festival, one such Judge was visiting the Nottingham Crown Court where I was appearing before a Crown Court Judge.

Nottingham robing room had a TV set in it. Every day I would engineer a break in proceedings to coincide with the running of the 3.30.

On Gold Cup day, Judge Tin Pot (not the same man as the other Judge Tin Pot, but a close relative), who had by now worked out what I was doing, was proving particularly difficult. Fate loaned a hand when a Juror asked for a comfort break with about two minutes to off.

As I arrived in the robing room, there with his legs up on a sofa was the High Court Judge, watching the race. Moral of the story: Judge with -itis – problems. Judge without -itis – no problems.

For the few with Judge-itis, is there a cure? Of course there is – you know who you are – be nice. STOP IT.

53.

Judges in lockdown

So how did the courts cope during lockdown? I suppose even the term is one we are not used to. We lock up, not down.

Did the wheels of justice continue to roll? I can only speak about the criminal courts, in which I have always dispensed justice and indeed from time to time dispensed with justice. The wheels came off.

What did we do? Old dogs had to learn new tricks.

The problems began as we were asked to work remotely; these were pastures new. My normal response to the question, are you interested in working hard, was, 'not remotely', but now my response changed.

As to my work ethic, good advice had come from a friend and colleague of mine, Renee Wong, who used to direct me, 'Don't work hard, work smart.' I don't know whether Confucius had said this, but Renee certainly had. And not just once but on every occasion I saw him. What he didn't say was, 'Don't work hard, work remote.'

Anyway, despite my great age, I had resolved to continue to work smart *and* remotely during the lockdown. How were the courts to continue? Like everyone else, they were on a voyage of discovery. What were the problems?

They were as follows:

Criminal trials stopped. It was quickly acknowledged that Jury trials could not be held remotely. Jurors in a Jury box do not sit two feet apart, never mind two metres. Traditionally, they work in pairs and share documents. A Jury trial is too much of an interactive exercise to be conducted digitally. People speaking in quick succession from different directions cannot be catered for remotely. Until they could reopen safely, trials were a non-starter.

That said, there was plenty of non-trial work to be done by the courts that could be heard via Zoom or its equivalent. When someone has been arrested and brought before the Magistrates Court, if he opts for a Jury trial, the pre-trial hearings have to be heard in the Crown Court. Perfect for the digital age.

REMOTE HEARINGS

The eagle-eyed among you would see difficulties straight away. Remote contact can serve a wonderful purpose; as a social tool during lockdown it was excellent. Not only could sequestered grandparents keep in touch, but a hundred people could join a meeting, each in their own little celebrity square. I did it myself. Everyone spoke at the same time. They all listened to your account of your health with feigned or no interest, while waiting the minimum period before they could tell you about their own health.

Unfortunately, remote court hearings require different skills and heightened cybersecurity demands an appropriate platform. It would have helped if the platforms hadn't kept changing. First there was Skype, then Skype for Business and finally CVP. To me CVP sounded like the very virus we were running away from, but turns out to stand for Cloud Video Platform and is a means to hook up the Judge, counsel, the court and the prison remotely. My understanding of these expressions was like that of a chimpanzee given a typewriter writing *Romeo and Juliet*. As it turned out, the platform that we used was as familiar to me as Platform 9¾ at Kings Cross going to Hogwarts School.

For me, technology was going to be an issue. Decisions had to be made. Where would I sit? I was told a darkened room was best, with limited light to spoil my screen presence. How would I dress? There was a strict code that I imposed on myself. Judicial robes for formal occasions; during the hot, early summer months I went for the debonair eccentric look – jacket and tie above the surface, swimming trunks and slippers below. After all, the court stands for the Judge, not the Judge for the court.

Problems were frequent, and I added to them. I took four steps forward and sixteen back. Getting on to CVP, for example, needed the digital cases system to be accessed to find the case; copying a link; opening Google Chrome and pasting it in; opening a web browser to connect to the hearing. At each of these hurdles I could and usually did fall. Easy for you to laugh.

But while a number of us, including me, were allowed to 'shield' for a time, the emphasis was on getting bodies back into court in person, rather than on screens or the end of a phone.

At least one senior Judge attended court with a measuring stick to see whether the courtrooms could be adapted and social distancing maintained. Personally, if I want my safety assured, I would ask the Health and Safety Executive to devise the way. I don't know about other Judges, but I know nothing of civil engineering and could no more redesign a court-room than build the bridge over the River Kwai.

STEADY AS SHE GOES

To look to provide a sanitised environment was, of course, a new culture for government buildings. As with hospitals, courts are not deluxe hotels, and there has often been no concentration on cleanliness. At the Crown Court in which I sit, I was privileged enough to celebrate the second anniversary of a particular fly's death. It had been hanging, suspended on a web, on staircase five ever since its tragic demise. To turn that into a Covid-safe zone was no small step for mankind.

FLORENCE NIGHTINGALE

Meanwhile, the Lord Chancellor was going down the route of opening new temporary courts. As the temporary hospitals for Covid patients who needed to be ventilated were called Nightingale Hospitals, these were Nightingale Courts. I can't see the link between the Lady with the Lamp and criminal justice, but you have to call the new courts something, and to call a court the Ronnie and Reggie Kray Home for Restorative Justice is probably pushing it a little.

But slowly we got back to work and, as we did so, this created an imperative to get people back into the buildings. In doing so, the MoJ wasn't merely swimming against the prevailing currents of mixing work between office and home, but could be accused – with some justification – of a lack of consistent thinking.

From the 2010s onwards, the courts were told that they should make use of technology and conduct ever-increasing numbers of virtual hearings. Everybody – the judiciary, bureaucrats and lawmakers – thought this was the way to go. A case in point was prisoners being produced at court. They do not want to be woken in the early hours to be put into a sweaty 'horsebox' (I exaggerate – a little) and driven to court for a short or ineffective hearing. This is not them being precious, but it is a disturbing fact that they could be brought in the morning from one prison, accompanied by all their belongings, and sent back to another at night. Plus for 'Category A' prisoners (potentially the most dangerous), security arrangements lengthened the process. So prisoners would welcome remote hearings where possible.

As for counsel, their fees having been reduced on so many occasions, they might earn a derisory fee less travel expenses and clerks' fees for the day's work. They too would happily forego attending such a hearing at court.

OUR KNIGHT IN SHINING ARMOUR

Why have I reviewed what has happened to the courts during the epidemic? It is to revert to our old friend and saviour, the Jury.

Once again, the advantage of the Jury system over a 'judge-only' system has been considered.

The lockdown period shone the spotlight on the two options. Again the popularity of keeping the Jury has far outstripped the competing view. The Criminal Bar Association has said it must be maintained. And whilst for a while, some toyed with the idea of reducing the current number of twelve jurors to nine or seven, to more easily and safely accommodate them, the enthusiasm for the Jury system is such that – just as there is always a majority against bringing back the death penalty no matter how many parliamentary debates are held – so, too, a majority of the legal profession will always vote to retain our St George: the Jury system. After all, injustice is a dragon, and dragons need slaying.

What have we learned? Jury trials in court, remote hearings for a decent percentage of the remaining cases.

Yet again, Covid saw advocates becoming the government's fall guys. Things went from bad to worse. Unassisted by furlough schemes for the self-employed, some barristers' chambers ceased to exist, and many advocates' dreams ended in a nightmare. When will they be properly protected?

PART 12

Life on the bench

54.

A light touch

As I have explained, it is far more likely that a guilty man will be acquitted than an innocent one convicted, and that is the way the system is designed, giving the Defendant the benefit of any doubt that happens to be passing along.

The chief priorities of a Judge should be independence, impartiality and the wish to influence ordinary people's lives – as well as lunch.

How does one broach the task? With a smile and kindly way.

A really important characteristic of both Bar and Bench is the desire and ability to bring calm to what might otherwise be a totally fraught situation. If, after this many words, you can remember the point of the book, it is to acknowledge that, whilst a Judge probably starts with an antipathy towards the Defendant, it's how he ends up that counts – making sure he does not skew the proceedings against him. I hope it is clear that I am compassionate, but am I, and my brother and sister Judges, fair and impartial? Even fair and impartial are not the same – one can be fair and not impartial, and I suspect that perhaps that is the best most of us can do.

We have considered how we have arrived at this point. Because of the occasions we see the system being beaten, our instinct may be to try and balance things out. But we must, and most of us do, fight it. We do this as Judges by constantly scrutinising our behaviour. Where a case, as is often the position, is one person's word against another, if we form our own view of where the truth lies and it is in favour of the victim and against the Defendant, we must behave as if we were a horseman with reins and steer a straight course. Just watch *Ben-Hur* and see how he steers his chariot away from Messala's spikes in the epic race. This should be the reaction of any Judge finding himself off-track.

Whilst fearlessness is the ultimate barrister's trait, for the Judge it really is about maintaining control. 'Some do it with a bitter look / Some with a flattering word.' In fact, it's done with a smile. A light touch.

A hands-off approach is so important. One tip I did adopt from the Reverend Watling mentioned previously: he had a handwritten sign on his desk saying 'keep quiet'. A Judge says something useful ten per cent of the time, useless sixty per cent of the time and thirty per cent of the time they cannot resist saying something. (Like ingredients for banana loaf, those measurements are approximate.)

As for the light touch, I had an ex-member of chambers come before me in his eighties. This was Robert Flach. His mobile phone went off. Into the thirty per cent category comes the Judge that makes a fuss. People are in and out of court so frequently; how are they always to remember to switch off their phones?

Robert's phone rang, and of course he looked for it in a flustered way.

'Don't worry, Mr Flach, and take your time.'

As he patted himself down he responded, 'Thank you, Your Honour. Mind you, I am so glad anyone still wants to speak to me.'

The real test of a Judge's fairness will come when he sums the case up to the Jury.

The order of the proceedings is that after the evidence comes the Judge's summing up. Recently it has been deemed appropriate that it is divided into two parts.

Part 1: The Law – the Judge tells the Jury what the law is, both in standard principles, e.g. how the Crown must prove its case so that they are sure of the Defendant's guilt, before moving on to the ingredients of the crime.

Let's look at an example. For theft, the Crown must prove:

a Taking.
b Property belonging to another.
c With the intention to permanently deprive the other of it.

d Dishonestly.

(That pretty well exhausts my legal compendium.)

I compile this summing up as we go along, and will provide the Jury with the directions in type. There is no room for bias.

When I tell the Jury that they are allowed to draw inferences but not to speculate, I sometimes smilingly recall the example given by Peter Greenwood from Chelmsford:

'Inference': If you see the fridge door open, a tub of cream spilled over the floor, and pussy sitting there licking her lips with white liquid on them, it's a fair inference that the cat has had the cream.'

Of course, by the time Peter had referred to 'pussy', counsel's row was awash with giggling.

After this part of the summing up there are then closing addresses from counsel for each side.

In Part 2, the Judge reminds the Jury of the facts of the case. Many think that, as the facts are a matter for the Jury anyway, there is no need to remind the Jury of them. I don't agree. If done fairly and succinctly, it is helpful.

The Jury retire to consider their verdict. They return and announce it. You don't agree with it? Tough.

55.

Views from the Bench

Sitting in the Judge's chair is like driving an SUV, except with more power. You see everything and everybody. When I took the job was the first time I realised that I must have driven Judges crazy with my often silly behaviour.

As is only natural, as the case proceeds I form my own views about the evidence and the witnesses. After all, trials are still human affairs. An example recently of a rape case I tried, concerned a man who had set up home with a woman whom he had met and paid as a sex worker. I had no doubt of her sincerity (again, not the same as truthfulness – complicated, this word stuff, huh?), and indeed I preferred the truthfulness of her account over his. The Crown's case relied on her evidence.

You might think that where a sexual relationship had been consensual and money-based, to then allege rape would be difficult to substantiate.

I was concerned, as I heard the two accounts, that I was against his rendition because he was the Defendant. But, as I listened, I realised this was not the case. She was simply the more credible witness, which means not just from what she said, but the way in which she said it. In short, I believed her.

When it came to sum the case up, fairness demands the Jury is assisted by the Judge's impartial directions. The Jury must not make assumptions. For instance, that the relationship, which began as prostitute and client, did not mean she could not be raped, and that consent to sex can be withdrawn at any time.

A Judge's view is not relevant, unless the Jury happen to share it. If they perceive that the Judge has a view and don't agree with it, they must dismiss it. That is the law, and that is what the Jury is told.

There is also the reality that, whilst about 65 per cent of allegations come to trial, the acquittal rate for rape allegations is at 35 per cent. And acquit is what they, the Jury, did in this case.

I think it only fair to add at this very late stage that, of the statistics mentioned in this book, I have invented 26 per cent of them.

SILENCE IS GOLDEN

The court is usually a place of an imbalance of speech and volume. Some lawyers, as previously described, have particularly attractive or beguiling voices. Like the snake Kaa in *The Jungle Book*, they use them to draw a Jury into their coils.

Many Judges like the sound of their own voices. Perhaps they find an authority in court that they did not previously have in the profession, or do not have at home. On the other hand, the Jury says nothing. As an advocate I used to say it was very odd, as in truth we never actually knew what they were thinking, though the odd silent yawn or snigger might provide a clue.

An unusual twist to the usual case came when I tried a deaf and mute person for seriously assaulting a person who was also deaf and mute. The court had to have a number of signers to translate. Thus counsel would ask a question, which would be signed for the witness and announced to the rest of us, and the witness would sign an answer, which likewise was translated by another signer.

I have only recently realised that sign language is so important, as those deaf or mute since birth will not necessarily have English as a first language.

I found the process fascinating, as I had not encountered it before.

The Defendant was convicted by the Jury. I would have had to send her to prison, but her mental state meant this was inappropriate, and an alternative route had to be found. To impose a Hospital Order under the Mental Health Act requires evidence of two doctors that she qualified by her condition, and a bed or place was available in a unit. This I imposed, and was surprised at how grateful and chirpy her response was.

I dare say all Judges have their particular peccadillos; mine is domestic violence.

I did a substantial number of such cases at the Bar, invariably, although not exclusively, man against woman. I guess it is the combination of bullying, cruelty and subverting of free will that offended my sensibilities, apart from the physical harm that might be caused.

Fortunately, its infinitely varied nature has now been catered for by one of the more necessary pieces of legislation, the crime of coercive and controlling behaviour.

It could be called the 'they'll grind you down' crime, as one partner wears away the resilience and resistance of the other. But the Jury know it when they see it, and if ever anyone needed an example of it that captivated a nation, it was the storyline of *The Archers* where Peter the bully wore down Helen the delightful. Without the addition of that statute, women could find themselves in the position of the woman who finally uses the knife on her persistently violent or domineering husband.

Occasionally, the position is reversed.

A court usher was killed by her husband. It may be because she tended to be listened to by everyone at court that he demanded to be listened to by her. Nobody doubted that she ruled the roost, and nobody doubted that he may have been driven to distraction and beyond.

In the end I was instructed to accept that this was not murder but was manslaughter.

My abhorrence for domestic violence cases is reflected in my sentencing, although of course that has to fall within certain guidelines.

Also, in bail applications where safety requires that I do not grant bail if I am sure there is good reason to believe that he will further assault her. I remember vividly my days at the Bar when the next time I would hear of the case was when the next step was murder.

56.

Do you want to be in my gang?

Although Judge selection is a random process in this country, it was partly on the basis of my experience in multi-handed (more than one accused) conspiracy trials that I was the assigned Judge to try three warring gangs, imaginatively known as 'A', 'B' and 'C'.

Predictably, the war was over the distribution of drugs, mostly cocaine around Bedford. The evidence consisted of recovered weapons, mobile phones, cell site analysis, car movements, eye witness and DNA. In other words, all of the evidence of a contemporary trial.

The weapons pointed to one man as the armourer for one side, whilst, as is so typical in modern trials, the mobile phones recovered acted as:

i.   Diaries – on any given day. All recovered phones are interrogated (as it's called) – their directories of names, nicknames, numbers, calls.

ii. Photogragh albums – Where available showing group photos, group selfies, maybe with weapons, on the bonnets of cars looking like motor show models.

iii. Tracking devices – seeing the movement from cell site; every call triggers a radio mast. Depending on the local topography, will tell the tracer how close to the mast the phone may be.

iv. Cars crossing borders on any given day will set off an ANPR machine, which monitors the car's registration

v. Conversations between one person and another. The number of conversations between one Defendant and another will give a good clue as to what is going on. Gang members tend to ring each other more than a dutiful son calls his dear old mum, doting husband his wife, and ardent lover his mistress, added together.

vi. Equally, the number of mobile phones one owns is a giveaway, as in:

Whilst two mobile phones indicates he's having an affair, three mobile phones equals he sells drugs.

Finally, on the phones were the video recordings of rap music, of the grunge variety, rapping about guns, violence and money. In short, everything the cases were about.

On reflection, not much in this trial of 2018 resembled a trial of 1978. Whilst there was little compelling eye-witness evidence, instead we had acres of telephone evidence.

I would like to say that the level of violence has gone down. But in the tale I told of the trial where the juror fell in love with the Defendant, the Defendant had shot a man's leg off. In an Old Bailey trial a semi-automatic had killed a pregnant woman; here the perpetrator of a machete attack had virtually severed a man's arm.

The trial was like being back at the Bar for me. Serious crime. Each Defendant had two advocates, so they could divide up between them the large amount of material and share the advocacy.

Things got off to an unusual start. Counsel was leading for the prosecution and, as he is charged to do, began to tell the Jury what the case was about. In the course of his opening the prosecutor did a remarkably stupid thing. He had one of the recovered weapons brought into court, and rather than just show it to the Jury, unbeknownst to all of us, he had it hidden under his desk. In a moment of 'high drama' he brought it out, cocked it with one arm, like John 'the Duke' Wayne and pulled the trigger.

It let off a sizeable clunk. Two of the Jury parted company with their skin.

I put my eyes back into their sockets: 'What do you think you are playing at?' I asked. My tone frightened even me. The prosecutor made the mistake of failing to recognise a rhetorical question, trying to provide an answer where none could do. He, as all the other counsel in the case, in fact was highly competent. His better judgement unfortunately left him for a moment. Whilst I am unrelated to monarchy, I treated him to a right royal something. He had pulled his last stroke, and everyone behaved thereafter.

The case occupied a lot of press space, not just for the seriousness of the crimes, or the sentences passed, but their topicality. Each act of violence by one team was followed by retaliation from the other: tit for tat. For each tit there was a tat and for each tat ... well, you've got the idea.

The escalation of the feud had followed the first act of kidnap and violence. The retaliation was by stabbing and a shooting.

Not only were the crimes typical of our time, so were the areas of evidence thrown up by the trial.

The previous convictions of some included conspiracy to kidnap and GBH with intent, but the most frightening piece of evidence was a recording released on YouTube of one of the teams going to relieve another gang in the Midlands of a quantity of drugs.

On their way back to Bedford they told their tale by rap, identifying themselves and boasting of what they had done.

The second trial resulted from other gang members looking to fill a vacuum. Violence sprung up to fill the gap left at the top of these gangs after the previous leaders were arrested and taken off the streets.

The sentences too reflected the fatigue of society with such crime, and involved my passing sentences including twenty years and over in some cases down to eighteen, nineteen, twelve in others, with a couple of non-custodial sentences (minor players).

57.

Parents and children

I have always looked on fascinated at the reaction of parents to their children's crimes and misdemeanours.

Throughout criminal history, the role of children has been a special one. Since Bill Sykes put Oliver Twist through the narrow space and into the house to be burgled, youngsters have been objects of abuse and exploitation.

Babies have been shaken, literally, by those who are supposed to care for them. A little older, their photos are to be leered at by any adult who might range between hopelessly inadequate and a fully fledged irredeemable paedophile.

Then their role as the perpetrators of crime, children committing the same crimes as adults, perhaps more readily associated with drug users and knife wielders – the courts have been enormously sensitive as to how they are dealt with, and of course I have followed that guidance. The principle in giving evidence is that if they can be classified as vulnerable, as with other witnesses, their evidence can be given either via a video link or behind a screen shielded from the alleged perpetrators.

I as the Judge will go and be introduced to the child, wig in my hand unless the sight of my head without my horsehair bonnet is too frightening.

Finally, in sentencing there is clear guidance from on high that, owing to the role of immaturity, discounts of a half or indeed two thirds can be made for a young person, with the aim being not to incarcerate where it can be avoided.

But what I have found interesting is the role of parents when their children are at court. To me there is nothing more usual, and indeed touching, than when a parent comes along to support them.

I once represented a Defendant known as the Chelmsford Rapist, who had stalked and raped a number of young women. His mother came every day to Chelmsford Crown Court. She could not face coming into the courtroom but sat outside of it in the vestibule every day of his four-week trial. Arriving at 9.30 a.m., she sat in the same place til 4.30 p.m.

And whilst of course a parent's attendance is not a 'get out of jail free' card, as a Judge I can be touched by the loyalty of a parent, which may be the thing most likely to stop their child reoffending.

So it is that at every sentence hearing, if a young person is attended by a close relative and I am on the border between sending him to prison or not, I might ask them if they wish to address me about what they think the right thing to do is.

Then in my sentencing remarks, if I am prepared not to send them to prison, I will always warn 'remember, if you do reoffend you are not just letting the court down, but you are responsible for the most enormous betrayal of your mum/grandma/brother/sister/aunt. (Note: No more than two relatives may be used as part of mitigation.)

58.

Doing the math

With the decision-making process being for the Jury and the power of the Court of Appeal to review cases that the Judge has got wrong, there are checks that will balance any maverick-type behaviour on his/her part. But the one area where the Jury will play no part is sentencing, be it a small fine or a sentence of life imprisonment.

Sentencing in the gravest crimes is really not that complex. It is, however, a little formulaic. The Court of Appeal expects us to pay strong heed to guidelines. You are to look at two general headings: Culpability (responsibility) and Harm. Then move them up or down, dependent on whether they are of good character or bad character, along with any other aggravation/mitigation.

So it might be as follows:

Grievous Bodily Harm

Culpability A Harm B

Bracket nine to sixteen years, starting point twelve

Up say to fifteen years if a bad record, down to ten if he has none.

You'd be tempted to say it sounds like: Think of

a number one to ten; double it: add a quarter of it divide by four.

In real life the process is too formulaic. The public would say it comes out too lenient. Remember you also get a third off for a guilty plea, plus the fact that by and large you only serve half. When I say you, I don't mean you, good reader, but 'one'. It is those facts that brings the process into disrepute, as sometimes it is barely worth the Defendant being checked into prison before it is time to check him out again.

Let us consider an everyday example that you know leaves you fuming. Burglary. The reality is that nine out of ten of us have a view as to what sort of punishment is appropriate. Thumb screws, deportation to Australia and running reruns of the *Sound of Music* nonstop day and night for two months being out of the question, let's settle on prison as appropriate. You will have an end figure in mind, say three years, and that's what you want him to serve.

But the sentencing process can go rapidly downhill, gathering no moss. If there is some mitigation, we will reduce that three-year starting point. So now we are at thirty months. He has no previous convictions, reduce it further to twenty-four months. He pleaded guilty at an early opportunity – now it's sixteen months.

He will only serve half, as that's the rule.

So your three years in jail becomes eight months. Now that is a bog standard example, and is bog standard wrong?

Different criteria apply to sentencing at the upper end of crime. In the gang wars I have described they used machetes, shotguns and a Scorpion semi-automatic machine gun.

An innocent bystander received machine-gun injury and a house was shot up.

The activities started with a kidnap and stabbing; moved to almost hacking someone's arm off; and discharging a firearm, leaving pellets in a victim's skull.

Hence sentences were not light.

The regime used for sentencing in such cases are those that allow a Judge to extend a sentence by dint of the fact that the Defendant can be legally categorised as 'Dangerous'. These sentences remain long. The sting in them is that the Defendant will serve two thirds rather than a half.

When I read that Bernie Madoff received 150 years in prison, I was reminded of the oldest of all quips in the legal world.

'Mr Madoff,' says the Judge, 'you'll spend 150 years in custody.'

Madoff: 'But I'm sixty-five years old. I'll die in prison.'

Judge: 'Well, do as much as you can.'

WHAT'S YOUR BAG, MAN?

Although the question of sentencing is entirely up to the Judge, it is quite nice to involve the Defendant, either with his agreement or not.

So, the Defendant might have said to the arresting officer:

"I'll probably get a five stretch for this.'

If you decide that without help from the Defendant four years would be more appropriate, it seems a bit miserly to knock off the last year and disappoint him. May as well go the extra mile.

Defendants can also assist me in the sentence I am going to pass by the bag they bring with them to take into prison. Usually prisoners who have been on bail about to be sent to prison will bring bags with them as they enter the dock, as if they are sentenced to prison they will go straight from court.

If as a Judge you are torn between whether to send someone to prison or not, the sight of him bringing into the dock a bag, shows what he expects. It would almost be wrong to disappoint him.

Equally, you would be unnatural if you did not weigh the bag up in your mind's eye as if you're on the Easy Jet bag drop: 'Hmm, that looks like a nine-month bag.'

I may use the sight of a bag as a warning.

'From the size of the bag you have brought with you, I'd say you were expecting two years imprisonment. I'm not going to bow to your expectations, but to suspend the sentence. Find yourself here again and bring a three-year trunk.'

There is also a sentencing policy that would apply to juries, albeit I have not had to deal with it – yet.

Judges invariably make opening remarks to juries when they have been empanelled. It has traditionally been:

'Don't discuss the case at home outside of your number; if your loved one asks what you are doing tell him the Judge has said I am not to discuss the case.'

None of us have ever been there when the juror has told her 6'4" partner that the Judge has said mind your own business, and so we don't know if the reply is:

a Of course dear or
b Tell the Judge where to go.

But those directions have now been added to with words to the effect of: 'Not discussing the case outside of your number includes not consulting the internet by looking at Google or social media. The whole world is out there, so if for instance you were inquisitive you might want to see an address or a street, no doubt you could find it. *Don't.*' (What is actually in our minds is that if you googled the Defendant the first words you would find might be 'Slasher Johnston in court again for knife crime.')

I continue with my direction: 'This is not trial by internet. There have been a couple of cases when it has become apparent the internet has been consulted. I'm not trying to frighten you, but the consequences have not just been to terminate the trial at great cost and inconvenience, but the steps taken against those jurors have been very strict.'

If you think about it, this could bring our justice system down (and I am always amazed it has not!).

I propose to include in the price of this book 'The Idiots Guide to Judging': I hope you appreciate getting two for the price of one.

What not to do:

1. Don't be unfair. You're not prosecuting.
2. Make sure you are not trying to convict someone or everyone.

I don't find sending people to prison too difficult — where you have no choice it is pretty clear, it is just a part of Mike Turner's principle: 'Do right, fear no one.'

I would be troubled by Baroness Hale of the Supreme Court's observation that the duty to follow the law sometimes requires Judges to 'harden our hearts'.

The sorts of cases troubling the Supreme Court don't trouble St Albans Crown Court. Rather than principles concerning euthanasia, we more often become embroiled in principles of lunch. But unlike Baroness Hale we get the pleasure of frequently not sending people to prison, and whilst not being troubled with pre-2020 compatibility of English law with European Law, we effect people's lives enormously. The frequently used reference to 'life-changing injuries' applies to life-changing mercy.

59.

Time to adjourn

A change is as good as a rest.

For reasons best known to others and not me, I left the Bar at a time when my practice was great to take a steady job, missing many of the rewards of my previous life. Why? I have no idea.

I agreed to go to Luton in Bedfordshire, which I had been to no more than once or twice in my life. Why? I have no idea.

When my pal Mike Kay QC moved to head up the court at St Albans I applied to go with him. Why? I have no idea. Other than I am a very loyal person.

So what can we conclude? The grass is always greener. That change is always good. By and large it doesn't matter what we decide, so long as we decide something. The two fish in my Piscean star sign become exhausted swimming against each other.

There is always the opportunity to do good, wherever we are.

'You're the Judge, you've got all the answers.'

Yes. Not all, but I do have some to those posed at the outset of the book, and if you have read to here, you'll have worked them out.

Yes, we are cynical, and understandably so. But our professionalism ensures it does not affect our ability to do a good job. This sometimes comes at a personal cost, and so we must recognise the need for wellbeing support for those working in the fraught and stressful world of the criminal justice system. Wide diversity and better remuneration for those joining the profession must be striven for.

All of the above can be packaged to help answer the central question: can Defendants be assured a fair trial? The rest relies on our Jury system being maintained.

I have taken a couple of hundred pages to espouse the Jury system. I could do it in a sentence: Juries have the perfume of democracy, 'Judge-only criminal trials' the odour of autocracy.

The reality is that, fortunately never as a barrister nor rarely as a Judge is the decision mine. It is the Jury's, and we can safely let the burden of proof do its work. If the evidence makes a Jury sure he is guilty, he is guilty. If not, he's not.

As a Judge, the verdict is what the verdict is. Smile and thank the Jury for it. I am useless at prediction in any event. I used to go into court with my diary to see what date I was available to sentence a Defendant if he was convicted. Invariably, if I took my diary in he was acquitted.

As for Judges and barristers and indeed advocates generally, I hope I have portrayed them in all their human guises. Warts and all. This has to include how they fight the cynicism that they have grown up with, which I know and believe they do during every day of their working lives.

But one can forgive a Judge who feels a sense of hopelessness. Now, that Judge does not include the blinkered, ambitious Judge. Those Judges simply put their heads down and charge towards what they see as the finishing line. That line is illusory, and they will keep moving their own ambition, until they end up somewhere between Donald Trump and the Supreme Commander of the North Korean people Kim Jong-un. But they will not learn that enough is never enough.

Why do I say a sense of hopelessness pervades the rest of us Judges? And don't I really mean me? Because however much we can influence and change people's lives for the better, there will still be those to whom we know it is most likely we cannot make a difference.

Many stalkers will carry on stalking, many paedos will carry on paedoing, many drunks will carry on drinking and many drug users will carry on drugging.

We score limited victories. A thousand victories do not represent a solution, but they do represent a thousand victories. What can be more satisfying than a job that permits you to garner a reputation for courtesy, and kindness delivered with humour?

I remember how I would turn up at court, read the name of the Judge and my heart would sink.

My day had just become harder. I would hate to be that Judge.

The role of advocates, police, jurors, staff is difficult enough, why make it harder, when a bit of kindness and consideration can make it easier?

That is all we can do, and either that is good enough for us or it's time to do other things, and that is what I am going to do now. I wonder if the Wimpy Bar in Leytonstone has a vacancy? After all, they still owe me for dry cleaning my hipsters.

Notes

For those interested in following up some of the references in the book, please see the notes below.

PART 1. IN THE BEGINNING

The 'posh' school in Essex is Bancroft's School. The brilliant lawyer is David, now Lord Pannick.

Pink Candy shrimps were sold there along with aniseed balls for one old penny for four.

Volpone or The Fox was published by Ben Jonson in 1607.

The Playboy Club in the 1960s was situated on Park Lane. It is currently alive and well, living in Mayfair.

The trial of actor Sid Owen took place in 1994.

PART 2: THE INSIDE TRACK

Blind justice: The two prisoners put into the same cell were Richard Linford who killed the other occupant, Christopher Edwards, biting off his ear in the course of the violence. This led to the independent Coonan inquiry in 1998. Coonan concluded that there were a 'litany of errors' contributing to Edwards's needless death. The parents of the deceased were frustrated by being placed on the margins of the inquiry and eventually took the matter to the European Court of Human Rights (Edwards and Another vs United Kingdom 2002). The ECHR judgement established the right of bereaved families to be involved in an effective and timely investigation in certain circumstances rather than being left on the periphery.

PART 3: COPS AND ROBBERS

Heroes and villains: The Battle of Brightlingsea was waged between 16 January and 30 October 1995. Members of the public had become increasingly concerned about the conditions in which animals were reared, transported and slaughtered. Small ports such as Brightlingsea were used to transport livestock after the country's three main ferry operators introduced bans on live cargo. This followed mounting public pressure about the suffering of sheep and cattle packed into huge transport vehicles for excessive periods. There were two national campaign groups trying to help this cause; the Royal Society for the Prevention of Cruelty to Animals and Compassion in World Farming.

The high-ranking officer I represented was Assistant Chief Constable Markham.

Reg 7 – Minding your Ps and Qs: A disciplinary tribunal in 2001 followed two officers' suspension for alleged misconduct. They remained on full pay for five years and ultimately the press spoke of settlement figures of £1.25 million between them to secure their resignations. A matter upon which I cannot comment.

'The Comeback Kid' exchange was between a barrister and police officer. Counsel, for reasons that must be apparent from the account, was known as 'Gib-gob'. The officer was a senior Essex policeman named Clarke and the venue Southend Crown Court.

Top of the cops: This is a reference to Inspector Richard Block and Sergeant, later Inspector, Graham Bull. The case concerned what was known as a 'tiger kidnap'. In 1991 the family of the manager of Tesco were held hostage to ensure the supermarket in Copdock, Ipswich, could be raided. Judge Greenwood at Chelmsford Crown Court sentenced those convicted for up to twenty-five years, remarking, 'It is rare, fortunately, I find I have men in front of me who are not only wicked but also evil. The vile cruelty you showed when kidnapping ordinary decent people was without mercy, and you can expect little from me.'

PART 4: THE MIDDLE AGES

LOMF: The trial of the two ambulancemen was in 1980. They were named Nunn and Grimstead and preferred to cut the fan belt of the ambulance rather than attend the 999 call that summoned them. I did one other case where an ambulance featured: to escape his pursuers, the victim sought refuge inside the back of an ambulance believing it would offer him 'sanctuary' – to no avail, his murderers followed him in there, killing him with a golf club, knife and baseball bat.

Something in the air: The village of Coggeshall had eleven unsolved murders between 1983 and 1986.

White van man: In 2010, the driver Larkland May parked the van on Pudding Lane, which, due to the insufficiently applied handbrake, ran away killing two pedestrians. This was probably the biggest single tragedy since the Great Fire of London was begun in a bakery on the same lane in 1666.

PART 5: MURDER AND MAYHEM

Jelly Beans: at the time it was passed, a sentence of Imprisonment for Public Protection was lawful. In 2012, such sentences became illegal. Albeit that no other like sentences were passed, in 2019 prisoners serving sentences under that regime still numbered 2,400.

A little knowledge: The legal principles of joint enterprise and conspiracy to commit crimes highlight the second limb of the constituents of crimes, i.e. the state of mind of the Defendant which must be proved to accompany the act itself (such as the intention to kill or cause really serious harm).

But what of the intentions of those other than the killer himself, those who are his accomplices? Must they too have the same intention albeit they are not doing the same act?

This topic was considered at length in Jogee 2017 by both the Court of Appeal and the Supreme Court.

Relatively speaking: Sons killing fathers: In 2008, Michael Johnson pleaded guilty at the Old Bailey to manslaughter of his eighty-one-year-old father. He beat him and set fire to his bed. At the time the Defendant was suffering the changing effects of the drug Keppra on his epilepsy. His father was an art expert specialising in Delacroix.

The case was prosecuted by former D.P.P. Sir Allan Greene

Sibling rivalry: The decapitation case referred to was that of James Baigent in 2007, in which I led Lawrence Bruce for the defence. Even when the head was recovered, the body took twenty-four hours to identify.

A pinch of salt: The six-week trial (late 2004/early 2005) of the salt-poisoning case at the Old Bailey is reconstructed on film produced on You Tube entitled *Real Crime: A Deadly Secret* in 2010. The Defendant's name is Petrina Stocker.

The worst of the worst: The man who savagely killed his partner and child was David Oakes. He received a whole-life sentence, the lawfulness of which was reviewed by the Court of Appeal in 2012. They found that to imprison someone for life without the opportunity for parole did not offend against European law. Shortly after his appeal hearing and having shot away half of his own face, he died of cancer.

PART 6: PICK'N'MIX

Taking the blame: featured the death of an elderly couple, Richard and Alice Orr, both in their 80's, from a gas explosion at their bungalow in 2003. The location was the housing trust Whiteley Village in Surrey.

Fraud – other people's greed: The Ostrich Farm fraud was tried in 2000 at Leicester Crown Court. Overall, the fraud was said to have netted the perpetrators £22 million – and a prison sentence.

Morality tales: Father Gerard Flahive was convicted of four counts of indecent assault and sent to prison for nine months in 2002.

PART 7: THE SCALES OF JUSTICE

Lock stock and two smoking barrels: In 1993 Barry Madle was working as a security guard at Leo's supermarket, Great Dunmow, when one of two robbers shot him in the leg. In 1995, two years later, he died from cancer.

At that time, and until 1996, it was the law that to constitute murder, death had to occur within a year and a day of (in this case) the shooting. Mr Madle's family believed that they had been denied justice as death had occurred outside of the prescribed period albeit they believed the shooting was linked to the cancer.

In any event, had Mr Madle died within a year and a day, the defence would have argued that the crime and the death were not inextricably linked.

One of the Defendants charged with armed robbery was sentenced to eighteen years.

Fate caught up with him, however, when, having been released in 2005, he was rearrested for a different murder and sentenced to thirty years in prison.

PART 8: CHECKS AND BALANCES

Faith: My last case at the Bar was the fraud on HBOS (Halifax Bank of Scotland). The BBC News, online 31st January 2017, referred to a highly unusual fraud case: senior bankers were convicted of crimes, including fraud and hiding the proceeds of crime, in the boom of irresponsible lending ahead of the 2008 crash.

Much to the detriment of the accused Bancroft, Mills and Scourfield were photos of them living high on the hog. Much to the credit of my client was the fact that he was not part of their 'crew'.

The case lasted for several months.

The inquiry that followed was chaired by Dame Linda Dobbs, the Counsel who was prosecuting the Defendant on the day the planes flew into the twin towers and who had featured in my professional life for forty years.

PART 10: TAKING THE QUEEN'S SHILLING

The phrase *to take the shilling*, or *to take the King's*, or *Queen's, shilling*, means *to sign up as a soldier*, from the former practice of giving a shilling to a recruit when he enlisted.

PART 11: HERE COME THE JUDGES

All of the cases referred to since I became a Judge occurred between 2017 and 2021 and have been tried by me, either in Luton or St Albans Crown Court. All of the gang trials have been covered extensively in the Press, for instance, the report in the *Bedford Independent* of 25 March 2019 entitled 'Warring Bedford and Kempston gangs now behind bars.'

Acknowledgements

I wish to say a particular thank you to Jim Ageros QC and his sister Jane McCready, who were early readers and guides on this book.

David Le Quesne with whom I navigated our years as law students. Valerie Charbit, Mike Epstein, Tanya Sless, Michael Rosehill, Karen Prooth and Robert Levy QC, who fed me inspiration whilst Maria fed me coffee.

Ian Bloom, legal consigliere who 'defamation' read the book.

Authors Tony Kent and Adam Leigh for their encouragement and Adam's introduction to whitefox. John Bond and George Edgeller, who flew with this.

Jack Smyth for the clever cover and Midas for PR work, particularly Hayley Cox.

The Criminal Bar, solicitors, Judges and other advocates too many to name, who enriched my life and work. 2 Bedford Row, whose unrivalled reputation helped me to have the career that I did.